And Then They All Puked...

My Experience as a (Groupon) Montauk Charter Boat Captain

By active USCG Licensed Captain Jeff Nichols

Cover: Design by Dwayne Booth

Book layout by HumorOutcasts Press.

Published 2021 by HumorOutcasts Press

Printed in the United States of America

ISBN: 978-1-7372746-2-9

Dedication

To Andrea

Every word of this is true—I don't know how to write fiction. It can all be verified through emails, Coast Guard records, court appearances, lawyers' letters, summonses, articles, and even eyewitnesses.

Contents

Part One

Chapter 1

The Fishing, the People...the Internet

I was not always a charter fishing boat captain. Upon graduating from the Merchant Marine Academy in '89 (Long Island branch, Kingpoints) and completing my tug and barge intern training on the Gowanus Canal in Brooklyn (summer of 1990, boy was it hot), I was assigned to pushing civilian cargo up the Suez Canal at the height of the First Gulf War. This was stressful for sure, but nothing compared to working in New York Harbor with its screaming current and narrow channels, or pushing a fifty-ton cement barge up through the Kenai Peninsula on the way to Anchorage, Alaska with its twelve-foot tides, or negotiating the straits of Gibraltar...

Wait. Are you buying this crap? This is the story I used to tell gullible customers on the way out to the fishing grounds. It was fun to watch their minds process this information as they took in my disorganized boat, tangled dock lines, and lying eyes. And when I told them I never went to the Merchant Marine Academy or the other places, we'd all have a good laugh. They might have believed me a little at first, but the smart ones did not buy it, it just did not add up.

The crux and motivation behind this book is to describe my experiences as the captain of a charter fishing boat, hopefully illustrating in a humorous way why I simply am not fit to take people fishing for money—even if the popular discount platform Groupon sent them. Many trips ended well, but a few ended with horrified customers, clinging and jumping for their very lives.

Just to fill you in, over the course of fifteen years running a registered charter fishing boat and taking people out to Montauk Point off the eastern tip of Long Island, I have issued five official Mayday distress calls and sunk two boats—with customers on them. I am far from proud of this. Luckily, every time, without fail, the Coast Guard came out, found us, and returned us to safety. They always did a great job and were always courteous. In the last case, last November 2020, the US Coast Guard had to pull me and my customer out of my swamped Boston Whaler. We were up to our knees in water, close to hypothermic, and the wind was picking up. I did not care so much about myself, or my lost boat, but I remember thinking, *this nice man, who just wanted to fish, is going to die.* It was 4:30, we had an hour of daylight left, and my cell phone was running out of juice. I knew Sea Tow wouldn't enter large seas in the dark. So, I dialed 911 and told the guy on the other end our predicament. Luckily, I was able to get the GPS coordinates to him before my phone died, and exactly one hour later we saw the lights of a small Coast Guard rescue boat. It took us 90 minutes on rough seas and against the tide at four knots to go the nine miles back to the harbor. Three of the four Coast Guard crew were new recruits from Oklahoma, 1500 miles from the nearest ocean. One of them said he "never expected to see anything like this." Another one started puking. The head officer, who was experienced, was able to get us back safely even though the dangerous area of water was known as the Shagwong Rip.

And that's not the worst example of my being unfit as a captain. In several cases, customers of mine ended up in the water. Looking back, some of these incidents were so outrageous they were almost comical, but make no mistake, at the time I did not think they were funny at all. Every time the Coast Guard plucked me and my customers off my sinking and unsafe boats and brought us back to the safety of Montauk harbor, I was always deeply mortified. Never did I think, *Wow! This would be a great story for a book.* After feeling badly for the poor bastard who had been on my boat, I'd make plans to leave Montauk for a while, or think about quitting the game altogether in disgrace.

The first time I ever sank a boat, it happened so quickly, I didn't even have time to call the Coast Guard. It was a late October day in 1989, and I was twenty-two years old. My stepfather had just bought a brand-new twenty-eight-foot Aquasport that he had generously said we could use, and I had word that "big gorilla" bluefish were biting at Moriches, by far the most dangerous inlet on Long Island. It's a long story, so I'll try to sum it up. When my friend Pete Heaphy and I got to Moriches, it was blowing close to 30 knots out of the south. I knew nothing about wind. I don't think I even knew that wind created waves. All I knew was that it was a gorgeous day and we were going fishing on a new boat—what could be better? Some guys on the dock told us not to go, but I figured we could head out of the inlet, and if it was bad, we could just turn around. Once we got to the inlet, we immediately encountered seven-foot waves, created, I now know, by the strong south wind against the outgoing tide. Beyond the waves, I saw birds diving in the distance which indicated that bluefish were chasing bait to the surface, and I knew I was not going to turn around.

It was a big boat, it could handle it, but after riding up and down several mountainous waves, we rode up a real screamer, probably ten feet high. When we slammed into the trough, all power went out in the boat. (Apparently a grounding wire had snapped.) My stepfather's new Aquasport would not start, and we were beginning to turn sideways. Two waves later and the boat was swamped and sinking. Pete and I took off our shoes and blue jeans and jumped overboard, right before she went down. We were now in the sixty-degree water being pushed out to sea by the outgoing tide. About a half mile out, there was kind of an eddy. I had lost sight of Pete, but I knew this was my chance to swim to the beach. I was pounded by the surf as I made my way towards the east cut of the inlet. Once I hit the beach, I was overjoyed to see Pete making his way in too. Luckily, my stepfather had insurance on the boat. My point is, if only I had taken this as a warning to stay away from boats, I would have avoided the carnage that is described in the rest of this book.

Fast forward a few decades and I'm now a captain, often taking calls from women who have purchased trips through the online discount platform Groupon for their husbands and sons to go fishing with me. These people are so hopeful they'll have a good time and are also laying down all the money up front, that I actually find myself rooting for them. Maybe these women think that catching fish together may somehow dissolve past resentments or misunderstandings between their men. Having done my fair share of father-son trips, I know that a fishing trip that's intended to bridge years of discord between a father and son rarely works, especially when the father is wearing construction boots and a camo jacket and is really into Nascar, and the son is a hairdresser who would rather be braiding someone's hair than fishing with his unsympathetic father.

Some of these trips went well, though, with lots of fish and laughs to be had, and I am proud and happy to have pulled them off. Some happy customers even felt the need (okay, I asked them) to go on the Groupon site and write rave reviews. But this book is not about those trips because happy stories don't sell.

By the way, you would be surprised at the people who shop on Groupon. Apparently even millionaires want a good deal. I was surprised by the number of Mercedes and BMWs that pulled into the marina, their owners with Groupon vouchers in hand. For Christ's sake, Chad Smith, the drummer from the Red Hot Chili Peppers, showed up with a fucking Groupon voucher.

When a Groupon salesman emailed me in the middle of February 2016, I really did not think it through. I was getting no calls, so I thought, what the hell? I did not expect the entire charter boat fleet to turn on me however. Take out Groupon customers and the Harbor gets very mad. The other captains said I was undercutting and degrading their business. They said terrible things about me and my girlfriend on the VHS radio channel 19, which is the one everyone with a boat monitors. I had to turn the radio down whenever I had customers on board so they wouldn't hear the comments.

After my fifth Mayday and third sunken boat, I hung up chartering for good. The war was over and I had lost. I was in AA at the time and trying to find a spiritual solution to my problems. I realized I was woefully underqualified to be a Montauk charter boat captain, so I took a job running the town septic boat and pumped out shit-filled mega yachts for twenty bucks a pop. I thought, *I really know the meaning of "below deck."* Point is, I spent ten hours a day in that harbor, and I saw the charter boat fleet boats tied up to their slips day in and day out, even on weekends. It broke my heart. I had become friends with some of these guys, and I wanted the fleet to survive, even though most of the captains did not like me.

Why weren't people fishing in Montauk? Some say it was because of the oppressive fishing regulations. Others felt that people were too into video games and cell phones to want to go fishing. Many pointed to the horribly congested roads in the tony Hamptons where it could take two hours just to get through the "trade parade" of landscapers making their way back west after taking care of rich peoples' lawns.

I personally feel that it was internet dating that did fishing in. Think about it. Some run-of-the-mill, middle-aged schlep whose whole identity revolves around fishing with his friends, resigns himself to hoping he'll meet some girl at a wedding six months down the road. But along come the dating apps, and—eureka!—he has a seemingly limitless pool of women to pick from. My point is, the money he used to spend on charters and party boats, he now spends trying to get his fat ass laid. He becomes obsessed with these now accessible women, like he used to be about catching fifty pounders, so he drops fishing by the wayside and sells his rods, only to reemerge at the docks ten years later, fifty pounds fatter, married with stepkids, and completely miserable.

Anyway, here is why *Groupon* was good for me. Yes, I would only make $275 for a half-day trip. Groupon charges $500, takes the money the day the voucher is bought , then immediately pays you between $175 and $200, which is nice to have in the middle of February when fishing season is months away. After the trip, they release another $75. But you have to put out for bait and gas in August and you've already spent the money. So you can't even make the trip without borrowing money. But that's a worst case scenario.

You can make different deals with Groupon on your cut and also raise your rate, but Groupon won't budge on a 50/50 split, even though it's your boat and you're doing 99 percent of the work, and you're paying the expenses. But the truth of the matter is, Groupon comes up with customers and that's the most important thing.

The Groupon demographic, if there is one, it is largely middle class to lower income people. Groupon people are usually polite and disciplined, at least the ones I've met.

Most charter boats are six passenger and run on single screw diesel engines. They run to the fishing grounds at around 10 to 12 knots.

What the other captains didn't get was that my phone was ringing and theirs were not. Often I'd be doubled booked with poor fucks waiting in the parking lot at 5am while I already had people on the boat. I'd offer to find them another boat. *Moondance* always gave me a hundred dollar kickback, which I deserved. I also sent plenty of people to the party boats, and then to the Clam Bar on the way home. Many of these customers return to Montauk year after year. They rent rooms and dine out. So, yes, that's right. Jeff Nichols was good for the harbor after all.

Sometimes I'd go around Groupon completely and tell the customer to pay me the $500. They would often re-book three times that season. That's $1500, so who says Groupon doesn't work?

*

In the early 90s, before the internet and way before Groupon, I would try to book trips through what now seems like a pretty onerous process. It's worth recounting, just to explain how things have changed.

I'd call the chambers of commerce in Montauk, and they would send me a bunch of brochures. When they arrived, I'd gleefully spread them out on dining room table and fawn over them. I admired the gorgeous lines of the boats. Some were custom sportfishing boats with names like *The Vivienne, Windy, The Adios*, The *Ada-k, The Hooker, The Blue 4.* Then there were a few assemblyline Hattaras and Vikings, style with bridges. The majority of the boats were downeast style: BHM, JC, West Macs, Holland, Osman Beal, Northcoast, Webbers Cove, Fortier. Others were simple lobster boats that had been converted to charter boats.

You couldn't tell much about the captains from the brochures, so word of mouth was the best way to find out who was catching what at a particular time. In addition to being a skilled and safe captain, it also helps if the guy is personable or funny. Captain Mark Morose was a good example,. Not only was he a remarkably skilled fisherman (not just some weekend warrior), but he was was funny and engaging, and people wanted to be around him, so he was booked all the time.

Only 25 percent of Montauk's fleet consists of full-time fisherman whose sole income comes from fishing. Most of the rest are part-timers, retired guys with pensions, or businessmen who want to write their boats and businesses off as a loss. I was one of these guys.

Truth be told, even though I had logged a legitimate amount of "seatime," I still did not consider myself a man of the sea, worthy of the title "captain." Theorize on this with me for a minute: what does that word "captain" represent in the context of maritime history? Let's think about all the captains on war ships, cargo ships, whaling ships. These guys spent *years* at a time at sea, in wooden boats, enduring brutal gales and hurricanes, with no radar, GPS, or satellite radio. They were the kind of men who were willing the pay to ultimate price of going down with the ship. . Imagine the pressure that came with the title of captain back then. For fuck's sake, half of their crew were probably plotting mutiny! I, on the other hand, had paid $750 for a three-week online course without anyone ever asking me to back a boat into a slip. There was no driver's test, and yet I was now a captain. Sure, I was a fishing enthusiast with a big heart, but no way should I be grouped with real mariners from the past or present.

Let me put it this way: if I happen to be sitting next to a real water man at a party, like someone who runs a dragger or longliner or builds dams or hydro windmills, I don't tell him I ever fished for a living. I'm too embarrassed. One time on an airplane, I happened to sit next to a guy who was an underwater welder headed to fix a spill on an oil rig. This mother fucker would dive down two hundred feet to patch a hole in an oil rig that was on fire and leaking oil. After he furnished me with all the wild details, he asked me what I did for a living. Feeling like half a man, I told him I was a golf caddy. It just shot out of my mouth. I did not feel comfortable calling myself a charter boat captain. I still don't.

There are also the weekend warrior boats. Many are run by skilled fisherman, but they are usually hobbyists. They make their money in some other profession and their charter business is either a tax write-off to supplement the huge expense of running a boat, or they simply want to "play captain." This not to say that you won't have fun and catch fish with them, but they're part-timers at best. I was one of these guys and knew it, but I was having so much fun, I didn't give a shit. I was possessed with catching big striped bass and mako sharks, and I needed people to help pay for it, so that's why I chartered. It wasn't about my clients having a good (and safe!) time; it was all about me and my fucking ego. As long as I could catch fish the way I wanted to when I wanted to, I did not care what people thought of me.

I would call the captains for their availability, and they might call me back around 6 or 7pm. It was not easy to get everyone together. Anyone who's done this knows it's no small feat to assemble trips.

Most of the trips I describe in this book are nightmare trips that went horribly wrong. Let's face it, there's nothing funny about a successful trip. To me, when the boat *Captain Crunch* went down three summers ago, and frantic customers scurried to the bow of the boat and dove off the pulpit for their lives, to be pulled out of the water by recreation boaters, who, thank god happened to be in area... that was funny. As Alan Alda's character proclaimed in Woody Allen's *Crimes and Misdemeanors,* "If it bends, it's funny. If it breaks, it's not funny." I chose to see the rescues as funny, largely because no one got broken.

*

I have always loved to fish, love everything about it. Still do. I like cutting bait, or the anticipation of the rod going off. I like the unique camaraderie largely between men. I like the ice, filleting fish, the birds diving for the scraps... I like it all. Even the time I put together a group friends in 1990 and we went out for giant tuna that were apparently sighted in an area called the CIA grounds in the Block Island Channel, about fifteen miles off the beach. We got skunked, but I was undeterred. As we were getting off the boat I overheard the captain say nonchalantly, "Well, maybe we will get them tomorrow." I remember thinking, *This guy gets to go again tomorrow! What a job! I've got to break into this world.*

Instead, I went back to New York City and pursued other things. I tried selling photocopiers and teaching school, but while doing so I thought only of Montauk.

In 2003 I sold a movie script and bought a small boat in Montauk, a twenty-two-foot Angler. While out on the water, I used to turn on the radio and listen to the captains talk.

With a few notable and wonderful exceptions, like Ed Bedaduchi on the *Marlin Princess* and Joe McBride on the *My Mate*, all the captains sounded absolutely and decidedly miserable. I remember being shocked by this. How could they not be happy? They get to go fishing every day. Some guys wait months to go fishing for one day. These guys do it every day.

When I was out on my little boat alone, I would often hear a captain matter-of-factly say, "Okay, I got the word." What was the word? The word is when it's very rough out, and the customers start to get seasick, and the organizer of the trip throws in the towel, cutting the trip short, and the boat heads back to the dock. This captain was happy because he could go home early and cut his lawn or watch baseball. Some more devious captains would purposely take their boat into the rips, where deep water met shallow water or reefs. They'd keep the boat in this turbulent water to induce seasickness. There are no refunds for seasickness.

Back then, I didn't understand what would make a captain do such a thing. But after being a captain full time for four years, often doing three trips a day, and mating full time for three years, I got it. Many captains of long liners and draggers left commercial draggers for what appeared to be the easier life of charter boat fishing and after a year dealing with customers, they went right back to work on a deck dragger.

If you take away not being mechanically inclined (which, by the way, is the most important aspect of being a successful charter boat owner and operator), and take into consideration all the impressive catches I produced over the years for customers (keeping in mind that fish are the stars of the show, and no one can be a "great" fisherman if there are no fish), I would say that I was a good but not great fisherman. The great ones have an uncanny nose for fish. They know by watching the tide and current exactly when to stop fishing for one species and move to the next. They pay extraordinary attention to detail, from getting the customers onboard safely, to making sure all the lines are good, to taking care of the fish after they're caught. A lot of captains let the fish develop bacteria, which can happen quickly—even on a twenty-minute car ride, fish can begin to smell. You need to first pack the whole fish in ice, and then pack the fillets in ice for maximum freshness.

When I started my small charter boat operation in Montauk in 2005, I was terrified of the local charter boat captains, as some of them were second generation fisherman. Not wanting to piss them off, I hung a self-deprecating shingle in front of my modest boat with the words SECOND CHOICE CHARTERS. Below it read, "If the top guys can't take you. I will. Fish guaranteed/night fishing only." I was a bit of a one-trick pony then, good at catching large striped bass at night. I placed in tournaments, was featured in magazines, and had the largest bass (fifty-four pounds) landed in Montauk by a registered charter boat . On top of this, I was always on the leader board at Gone Fishing Marina, which was a storied striped bass institution where the best night bass fisherman in the business would keep their boats. (Bob Storke, of the infamous *The Caprice*, basically pioneered night fishing in Montauk in the early 70s. Bob Rochetia from Rainbow charters set a world record for this marina.) They would congregate at the docks after their night trips. I learned a lot from them.

I attracted a certain clientele. Trophy hunters came from all over just to catch striped bass. As I feared, the majority of the Montauk charter fleet did not like me, and one reason was because the big bass were biting at night, and the daytime bite was nonexistent. The captains would pronounce to their customers, "We can't catch what's not there." Then the customers would go on Noreast.com and say, "Well, Jeff Nichols got 'em last night." Then the captains would go online and see one of my customers gleefully holding a forty-five-pounder. I must have been doing something right, because the whole harbor was calling me "crazy Jeff" on channel 19, but when they said terrible things about how fat my girlfriend's legs were, I eventually turned the radio off.

Besides the trophy hunters, a typical Second Choice Charters customer was in his fifties, smelled badly, and smoked heavily. Many seemed to be perpetually waiting for some type of workman's comp. They insisted that I not put pictures of them on social media because they were afraid or being exposed as not handicapped. I called them "clients" the way a prostitute calls a john a "client." They were the type of guys who thought nothing of arriving at the marina, unloading their gear, and then taking a piss in the parking lot in front of people. After the trip, they'd get drunk and pass out in their cars and trucks. A successful trip was when these guys didn't steal my sinkers and fillet knives.

By contrast, the Groupon customers were much more well-mannered. They looked like they were about to go on whale watching trip, or a ride at an amusement park. They didn't seemed concerned that my company was called Second Choice Charters or that a Google search of my name would reveal there was a movie called *American Loser* based on my life. (Luckily most people did not see the film, which was originally titled *Trainwreck: My Life as an Idiot*.)

The Groupon customers never seemed to anticipate any problems like being hurled into the water and having to swim for their lives. They were, however, all concerned about how much Dramamine they should take it even though I clearly stated this on my website. I don't think I ever went over any safety equipment or protocol, even though we were headed out into the mighty Atlantic. (One summer when a charter captain spent ten grueling minutes to go over safety equipment on a tour of Loch Ness, I was like, *Okay, just drive this piece of shit and show us the sea lizard already*.)

These poor unsuspecting customers, with discount vouchers clutched in their hands, encountered a sunburnt, disheveled, poorly aging man with a filthy boat. I'd encourage them by showing them racks of dead fish from a previous trip. "Don't worry. Blood stains and flies means it was a good trip. No blood stains and you should be suspicious." Most bit, they wanted to go. Some had never been on a boat. Many had not been in years. And 90 percent would end up puking.

Not only was I a slob and my various charter vessels unsafe by any standard, I occasionally said and did inappropriate things on Groupon outings. They were not return customers and therefore unaccustomed to my brand of humor. Simply put, they were not fans of "Jeff Nichols, the label." They just expected a competent captain, and a seaworthy boat. Surely Groupon must have checked into my credibility before promoting me, right?

One customer kept asking me to videotape him reeling in fish. He was a nice guy and we were getting along great, so in a sophomoric spasm, I pulled down my gym shorts and zoomed in on my cock.

Later that night I got a text from him. "Why are your balls in my video?"

Chapter 2

Why would someone want to be a captain?

I get it. You're a good, maybe even a great fisherman. You have won a few tournaments. Maybe the idea hits you while you're strolling down a dock with your girl at sunset on Cape Cod, Block Island, or someplace more exotic like Costa Rica, Cabo San Lucas, Mozambique, or Mexico. You come around to a charter boat bobbing in a slip with a chipper mate still cleaning fresh mahimahi caught that day. You picture the captain living in a quaint house just up the road. You know that all of your 3000 Facebook friends would book trips with you and then...stop right there! This is an illusion.

Here is a simple fact that a famous Montauk captain told me years ago: just to cover expenses like gas, dockage, insurance, and advertising, you have to do forty trips before you make a dime. Let that really sink in. You may think all your Facebook and college friends will charter you, but they won't. They won't even go with you for free. Most importantly, if you are not mechanically inclined, you won't make it as a charter boat captain.

Charter fishing is commercial fishing—there is no real difference to other ways of making a living. You're working eighteen-hour days. You're not seeing your girlfriend (and you will probably lose your girlfriend), you're not able to go to weddings, or even walk your dogs, and now with cell phones the texting and phone calls are endless. Trying to a keep a mate is tough because they have to sleep in their cars as there is no housing in Montauk.

It is true that if you pull into a slip with a boat loaded with fish, or weigh in a nice mako, or better yet a giant tuna and happy customers, you do kinda feel like da mother fucka! But most charter boat captains burn out. Once you have to make money fishing, you enjoy it less; there's just too much pressure.

Once you have given it up, though you won't remember the bad times.

Even though I've caught some amazing fish: eight striped bass over 50 pounds, hundreds of 40 pounders, gotten huge tips, gotten laid, and made over 20 k in tournaments over the years, when it's all over this is not actually what you will remember. You will remember the laughs, but there will be even more subtle, very human and touching moments that just stick with you... you see man at his best.

For example, once when I was a mate on the *Nicole Marie*, we had 6 older, blue collar guys probably in their seventies, all retired, and they drank cheap beer like Pabst Blue Ribbon, or Genesee Ale. They got drunk, but there was also a subtlety about them. I saw this on many trips...maybe it has to do with the sea, but I was always struck by little gestures. There is a nice way that the men looked after one another, there is something as simple as the way the way the guy opens the cooler and offers the other guys a sandwich. They were not store bought, though that would have been fine, they were often handmade, wrapped carefully in tin foil. You could tell the guy probably stayed up late at night making them, he cared. And methodically handed them out to his friends. He even made one for the captain and me.

And these guys were funny. As they ate their sandwiches taking a break from fishing, one guy was bragging about how cheap he gets his cartons of cigarettes from an Indian reservation back west. They were all off brands by the way, like Clark, Lucky Strike and Salem. His brand was American Spirit. He was careful not to say which reservation as there were over ten shops off Montauk highway alone in Southampton but he got a carton for ten bucks! That's 50 cents a pack! He was not necessarily bragging, he was just announcing a good deal, yet there was a pridefulness about him that I liked.

On the way back to the dock after I had finished cleaning the fish, I wanted to make conversation—I mean I did not smoke, and even if I did, I certainly had no interest in procuring a carton of American Spirit cigarettes, no matter what the price. So, for conversation purposes, I asked the colorful guy on what specific reservation did he get the cigarettes at 6 bucks a carton. He looked at me and said in a gruff but playful manner. "What, now you want to know everything?" This struck me as so funny, as if he was scared if I had found out the name of the store I would go down there and buy every carton of American Spirit cigarettes. I began using this line myself, "what, now you want to know everything?" Often, it works well after you've answered a series of questions. Like, where did I catch those black fish? Happy to furnish the answer, I answer: Fishers Island. What type of crab did I use? Answer: Green crabs. Then they ask what time did the fish start biting and what tide—now I'd have the perfect set up for the line, and hit them with: "what, know you want to know everything?" Try it, it works...a lot of time they laugh, or they're apologetic.

While I'm at it, here's another good one you can use. You're driving your boat to the fishing spot, and your friend or customer is excited and chatting your ear off. In the middle of his next sentence, cut him off and say, "Hey, do you mind if we have a little quiet time?" Some old salt did that to me once and I never forgot it. "How about a little quiet time?" It's great, the person gets so offended, and really goes quiet or sulks.

These are the things that stick with me. They're amazing memories, but during the time I was on the water professionally, I couldn't appreciate them for all the other troubles I had.

Prior to Groupon, I was exclusively a night trophy striped bass charter boat captain. As my operation was called Second Choice Charters, I obviously did not get top clientele. Most of the guys were diehard striped bass fishermen like me.

But in 2016 I turned over to Groupon, booking trips through the online platform. When I was doing primarily Groupon trips (2016 -2018), I would fish in the daytime. It was a very pedestrian schedule (mornings from 6 to 11, afternoons from 12 to 4, twilight from 4-9). And you had to be exact if you brought a Groupon trip, if you came in 10 minutes early they may try not to pay. I had a couple of real knife fights in the parking lots trying to get paid.

I targeted all species, or whatever I could rustle up for customers: striped bass, blue fish, porgies, a few fluke, a few tuna, and occasionally a small keeper mako or thresher shark. Sea bass were prevalent and good eating. I could do it all, and when I was not calling in maydays, I was busy filling coolers for happy customers. Though Groupon may have bad reputation for cheap people, I liked all of them. They tip well. If you're planning to do Groupon, you may need a bigger boat. I did.

I don't know if Groupon represents a cross section of Americans, but if it does, there a lot of fat fucks out there. The average male American weighs 250 pounds.

Usually right before I picked up the customers at the loading dock, I would call the organizer of the trip and ask as nicely as possible, for docking purposes, if anyone was over 300 pounds. Then I would hear "Hold on captain...hey Ray...look, don't get mad at me, it's the captain asking, but what are you weighing in at? Oh. OK, captain there will be three of us, at least." One time I had 4 people over 400 pounds. Comedian Arty Lang wrote a book called *Too Fat to Fish*, but evidently this is not true, just look at any party boat. Then google "party fishing boats from the 1950s," every guy on the boat is skinny and well dressed; today, all fat fucks.

*

I ran my boat out of Montauk Point, a small but notorious town on the eastern tip of Long Island, NY. While it may not necessarily be a destination like Key West or Costa Rica, because it pushes out 120 miles out into the Atlantic ocean, surrounded by huge boulder fields, it offers great structure for fishing. It is at the very least a nautical reference point for most East coast mariners. Now at one point in time, the 1920s, through the 1950s, Montauk was dubbed the sport fishing capital of the world, and there was a legitimate claim in this. Who could argue,

considering in the 1950s on a given day on a charter boat like say Freddy Tumor *Dawn*, you could venture 15 miles off shore and land 6 giant tuna all over 700 pounds; then go weigh them in and as they had no commercial value because the Sushi phenomena had not taken off yet. You could give them away as crop fertilizer or cat food... or simply bring back out to the inlet and let them drift off dead for the crabs to eat.

Or you could go 17 miles and fill a boat with as many 50 pound yellowfin tuna as you wanted. There were no regulations. Just off shore lurked an abundance of large Mako sharks. No one would even think of bringing in a baby 160 pounder, why would they, when they could bring in 4 over 300 pounds? In the winter it was cod, plenty of 30 pounders and 40 pounders; huge stocks of sea trout (weakfish) ran with the abundant stripers and blues, and there were snow shoe flounder in the spring and even blow fish. Sure they probably had off years, like the hurricane of '38, and weather issues like we do now, but for the most part epic fishing was the norm, they knew no other way. In the 1920s sport fishing was only assessable to the rich, in the '50s the working class would pack on trains in Manhattan called the Fishagrala express. This is from a time long past, for now the interest in fishing and hunting is way down. Men seem to be more into cell phones and internet dating, for the most part. That old way of things is all gone now. I guess we can say at the very least our ancestors were not conservation minded, and at worst they were inconsiderate and greedy of natural resources, or as my cousin Kenny used to say when I registered my disgust as he gaffed his fifth illegal striped bass, "hey, ain't nobody saved me no buffalo." Perhaps this is the attitude that gets passed on…

But what was still left was the striped bass (the *Morone saxatilis*), America's fish. Though over the years, there've been huge dips in biomass population, unlike the cod fish, that appears to have not vanished in any significant way, due to conservation efforts and a moratorium on the fish in the 80s by all states. Abundant, at least when I got on the scene in 1995, were the striped bass the Morossaxton, the most respected, controversial and sought after sport fish on the east coast. With its gorgeous aligned stripes, who's to say it's not America's fish? It was only in recent years (possibly due to global warming) that stripers began to migrate past Maine up into Canada and into the Nova Scotia river.

My first memories of fishing are wholesome and wonderful. They started when I was around eight or nine, maybe ten years old. In the early '70s my sister, mother, father and I would make the pilgrimage up Interstate-95 from New York City and to my grandfather's enchanted summer home in Harwichport on Cape Cod. It was a sprawling compound of a house overlooking Nantucket Sound, probably built in the late seventeenth century. We descended on the house for two weeks every August. My poor overwhelmed grandparents sought refuge in their small apartment above the garage, Anne Frank style. It was rumored that behind one of the fireplaces in the main house was a hiding place where slaves hid during the Civil War. My always-curious mother simply had to see if this was true, and to me and my sister's delight (not so much my grandparents'), knocked down part of the fireplace. Low and behold there was a little room back there. As big as the house was with its expansive three sections, it was actually moved and in its place now stands a much bigger house. It is impressive but sadly a bit plain and ordinary and well... just too big.

While other kids hung out at the nearby Wychmere Harbor Yacht Club participating in regattas and sailing school, I was drawn, to the disapproval of my grandfather, by an unseen hand down to the public docks in town where I would show up at three in the afternoon to watch the charter fishing boats come in from fishing off "the shoals," the south side of Nantucket. Now granted, at that young age, everything appears cool and amazing. But to me, watching the happy customers scramble off the small Down Easter charter boats and the captains or mates unload fish after fish from huge boxes onto the docks, so spectators could ooh and ah over the mixture of big bass and blues, was nothing less than truly mesmerizing.

There were no limits in the early '70s; the more fish the better. The idea of fish conservation, let alone the practice of it, would not be established for another ten years or so. The customers would take what they wanted and then the fishermen would pull up in their Ford pick-up trucks and fill the back with fish. They would drive off to sell them. Because there was no ice they couldn't have been going far; maybe Thompson's clam bar at the end of the street. It seemed like such a wholesome and guilt-free activity, all so simple and natural. Who would think that in the years to come selling fish directly to restaurants would be illegal, causing a huge black market fishing industry to emerge, and fishermen to be labeled criminals?

I loved the smell of the docks: a mix of motor oil, diesel fuel, bleach and rotting fish. Our senses are so alive when we are young. Everything was thrilling at that age. Even a simple drive to a destination, or knowing it was Friday, was earth shaking, wasn't it? I remember an old girlfriend telling me once that when she was young she had to share space with her sisters. Once one moved out she was thrilled—actually thrilled—to have her own drawer to put stuff in! And to think, thirty years later and we are all guzzling down our Prozac with black coffee just to try and approximate a smile. Fishing for me—the concept, the mystery, the equipment, the tough looking captains, the industry of it all—was like the first time I was exposed to rock music groups like Kansas, Boston, and Jethro Tull. It absolutely blew my mind. I think I fell in love with Montauk as an adult because it had the same smell as Wychmere Harbor. Maybe boat soap mixed with decomposing baitfish baking on the hot wooden docks sounds like an odd thing to derive pleasure from, but I loved it and still do. It's analogous, perhaps, to the alcoholic's loving the smell of a gin mill - which is not as exciting for most people. I remember that all around the periphery of the parking at the docks there were little wooden fish shacks. Some of them were completely dilapidated with broken windows. I think those used to belong to the commercial guys because I remember huge nets, flags and orange buoys inside, all tools of the trade, when I peeked in the windows in utter awe.

I visited Harwichport a few years back with my dog Columbo. The docks themselves had less character and seemed fairly sterile - they got rid of the wooden docks and commercial boats (where were the lobstermen?) And they just had one cement pier. But to my happiness the shacks or fishing huts are still there now! With nets in them! One captain was particularly nice to me at the docks, Captain Bob, owner of the boat called the *OJ*. It was a small Down Easter lobster boat, between thirty and forty feet. I guess at one point I must have asked him if I could tag along one day. He must have said if it was all right with the customers and all right with my mom I could go. So my adventurous mom threw caution to the wind and brought me to the docks at 6 am. Captain Bob ran the idea by the charter, two nice couples, as planned. They gave me the green light, and we were off. It was a long ride to Monomoy Point and around Nantucket Island to the shoals, probably over thirty miles one way. For those slow boats it must have taken two hours just to get there.

Perhaps, if my first visit to these fishing grounds off this storied island had been on a nice clear day, my memory of the trip would not be so spectacularly vivid. It was foggy, pea soup, when we got to the fishing area; we could not see but we could hear seagulls and gannets diving and singing, trying to catch the disoriented baitfish jumping out of the water in their desperate effort to avoid being eaten by the bigger fish that preyed upon them. This was the very definition of wild. This was the food chain at work, big prey after little prey...and we were in the thick of it.

I remember the lures Captain Bob used. One was called a Hoochie and consisted of a plastic skirt pulled over what looked like a ball bearing chain. The Hoochie had a single hook on the end of it. He used different colors: green, red, orange, rainbow, and black depending what was working best. He had many of these lures. I remember being impressed by the clean, white-wax covered little cardboard boxes that were stacked neatly and filled with the Hoochie lures. This was very much a professional operation! As we let out the line, we would occasionally see another charter boat come through, then just as quickly, vanish back into the fog. I guess the captains were communicating by VHF radio, and maybe they had some type of locating system. How did they know where they were? I guess they were all lining up to fish a rip, trying to make the same pass. Then the fish started to come over the side, one after another.

I watched these men and women wrestle the fish, quietly encouraging one another - a few blues and then a big striper. Then it was my turn; how could they not let the renegade stowaway take a crack at it? I remember I had a fish close to the boat when the hook pulled out at the last minute. I watched helplessly as the bass drifted back under the surface. I did not catch this fish that day. Perhaps this failure, "the one that got away," stayed with me and worked on my subconscious, eventually creating an impulse to slaughter every fish I came across for decades to come.

Though I hated to leave Cape Cod at the end of our two-week summer vacation, I was lucky to be able to return to another fishing paradise. My parents had a country home just fifty miles north of NYC that was perched on an idyllic spring fed lake/pond in the Sedgewood Club, in Carmel, New York. I am not sure what distinguishes a pond from a lake, but it can't just be size because China Lake is small. It's maybe three hundred yards long and two hundred yards wide at best, but deep. Parts of China Lake hit sixty feet. When we swam near the bottom we could actually feel the spring coming up from the lake's floor, cold and strong. There were very few houses on the lake at the time, maybe nine. They were modest little cottages. None of them had big lawns and since they were primarily weekend places, septic problems were not yet an issue. In fact, we drank the water unfiltered. The conditions were conducive to supporting a healthy ecosystem. And a robust ecosystem it was. Sit a minute at the edge of China Lake in the '70s or '80s and you would basically see an aquarium swim by, schools of yellow perch, their cousin white perch, various sized sun fish and crappies and then the minnows also called shiners and saw bellies. Hundreds of scared quick-moving minnows grouped together to look bigger. And then, of course on cue, the minnows' nemesis, a big old largemouth or smallmouth bass, confidently moseyed by. You could not see the pickerel because they were hiding in the grass, or the catfish, because they stayed in deeper water. In the sandy areas of China Lake all you had to do was put a foot in the water to make twenty crayfish lunge backward with their tails in the air and resettle away from you in a confrontational pose, their claws up to try to frighten you as if saying, "Okay, bring it on!" As kids, we all loved to get plastic cups and try to catch these marvelously spunky little lobsters. There was also the occasional visit by a water snake, which sent all swimmers frantically swimming to the dock as if it was a ravenous great white shark looking for lunch. For days afterwards no one would go in the water after sighting a benign water snake.

At night we would go to bed with bullfrogs roaring, and crickets singing and thunderous splashing, presumably trout rounding up the baitfish. The fishing was great. The pond was stocked every year with trout: brook, rainbow, golden and brown. Just as we did in the charter boats off the Cape, we would troll for them. My dad and I would take our small aluminum rowboat (which occasionally leaked) and slowly move around the periphery of the lake. We constantly altered the speed of the boat to make the lure, either a Phips "Feebee" or a flat fish or a Rooster Tail, appealing to our prey. We also tried to place the lure in the water column where the fish were. I am sure a lot of it was blind luck. We had no fish finder or electronics of any kind. When we did it right we'd get the "whack." We had no rod holders so the light rod would go shooting off. Sometimes we would barely grab it in time with our feet before it had a chance to shoot off the side of the boat. One thing is for sure, I did not have ADD(which I was later diagnosed with) when I was rowing around that lake, my eyes glued to the tip of the rod waiting for the strike. In fact I was hyper focused.

When winter came it was time for ice fishing with my old friend Judge Dickenson, a Putnam County Supreme Court Justice. Sometimes the pond froze over by Christmas time. It happened quickly if there were freezing temperatures coupled with no wind. The next day a sheet of clear black ice would cover the entire lake. All you needed was an inch and a half to walk on, three inches to drive a truck across. You knew it was hard when it cracked and rumbled and moaned like a whale. While others occasionally fished on the lake, "the Judge" wore a distinctive orange hunting jacket. I would awaken around 7 am to the sound of drilling, look out my window and peer through the trees to get a glimpse of that orange jacket. Once I saw the orange jacket I would rejoice. I would bolt out of the house, my mother chasing me with a mitten or a hat or even a boot that I had forgotten in my excitement. I was a learning disabled young boy. I was always very sloppy and had a tough time in sports and at school, but something about fishing—the gear, the camaraderie, the patience, the anticipation and the thrill of the reward, the possibility of a trophy fish, all appealed to me. I would run across the ice, watching out for soft spots, and assist the Judge with skimming out the holes after he drilled them with his power auger. Then we would set out the tip-ups; we were allowed five each by law. It was a very simple concept: three thin pieces of wood connected by a bolt with a spool of line at the bottom and a piece of metal sticking out. If a fish took the line, it tripped a thin metal wire and made an orange flag pop up to indicate that a fish was on. This would happen five to ten times on a good day, none on a bad day. I would be sitting there talking to the Judge as he drank his homemade cider and fried up some venison that he had hunted in the fall. The conversation was always about fishing: his old friend Elmer's eight-pound chain pickerel, his grandson's ten-pound lake trout that he caught on Gleneida Lake in Carmel, and so on. It was always about big fish. The Judge liked me—how could he not like a kid that into fishing?—but he also liked having someone to talk to.

Then a flag would pop up indicating a fish had hit one of our lines! (Sometimes on a crisp day you could hear it snap before you saw it.) I would run over. Sometimes the entire tip-up would be shaking with a big fish. Sometimes the line would be screaming out—that usually meant a small or largemouth bass. Other times the line would be just sitting there out to one side or another—that meant a pickerel. Mostly we caught chain and grass pickerel and yellow perch. The Judge would make pickerel fish sticks and pickerel salad out of those, but occasionally we would get a nice trout.

One day, I was out picking up our lines to go home, and as I began to pull the line in, I was met with resistance. Something big and alive was on the end of the line. For some reason the flag had not popped up; it may have been frozen. I started to pull, trembling with anticipation. The scary giant hooked-jawed brown trout that appeared at the hole was more than I could handle. It had a huge eye that stared back at me. I screamed, and the Judge came running over. I gave the line to him, and he craftily negotiated the giant fish through the small hole. God, did we rejoice! The trout weighed six and a half pounds! My father got it mounted for me, and it proudly hung on the mantelpiece adorning the living room for many years before a tragic fire took it. This was it for me; from here on out I associated catching big trophy fish with unmitigated pride and pleasure.

Chapter 3

The nature of the striped bass fisherman

Most fishermen would target and like landing striped bass... they give a great initial run off, and the small ones can be eaten (though not as tasty as fluke, or black fish), but the big striped bass are basically inedible (metal laden, tough, gamey). I suppose a sensitive, smart man with his ego intact would try to revive and release a big female Striper whether it will lay eggs or not. If you're not going to mount it, why kill it?

I was not this man. For 20 years I was a trophy hunter, a cow hunter, a slob slayer... I targeted big breeding female striped bass and weighed them in for my ego's sake.

For 20 years I fished approximately 100 nights a year trying to catch the big one. I insulated myself in the striper world. I knew all the players: Montauk chartering legend Jimmy George with his secret spoon, Bob Stork, who had over 70 50 pounders, and Craig Myerson, the current world record holder (81 pounds).

These guys were idolized by a small and ever shrinking group of trophy Striped bass hunters; they are the Tom Brady's and Michael Jordans of the sport.

We were men usually over 40 whose entire identities revolved around trying to catch their personal best.

As most of my customers were striped bass addicts after all, who would stay up all night to fish, I think I am capable of drawing up a loose profile of a cow trophy striped bass fisherman.

First off, we are weirdoes. OCD, neurotic, narcissistic, isolationists. There is an entire subculture that revolves around landing their personal best, a trophy over 50, 60—or the holy grail, over 70 pounds. Peter Vican achieved this milestone twice, on a spinning rod no less, off Block Island, breaking his own Rhode Island state record of 77 pounds.

I cannot speak for any other boat. I can only speak about my customers, and why I hung the benign little shingle *Second Choice Charters* and the subtitle "If the top guys won't take you, I will." I did not get the top rate guys. Look, if I was a threat to your business with that motto then you did not have a business.

But I got diehards nonetheless, obsessed about beating their personal best. Most of them were obese, all over 50, most lived with their parents or a parent, all were blue collar, most were skilled laborers at one point, and, like I said earlier, many were waiting for social security disability settlements or a worker's comp payout. They were all waiting for the "check" and constantly talked about what they thought would be a payout in the high six figures. These cases never seemed to pay out. A lot of them got caught doing other jobs—one guy was getting worker's comp from the fire department and got caught on video, carrying a 100 pound bundle of shingles up a ladder. They did not want any pictures of them on Facebook holding big fish until they got the claim check. But it was always the big number never came. One brick layer had a beam fall over him. A younger guy was on his bike and got hit by cab; assuming a huge payday, he sat in his mother's basement for seven years expecting payout from the insurance company that never came.

Still they showed up. I was cheap, I cut deals too. They would go and make their money back by selling their whole fish to local restaurants and some nights I would get lucky and they would not steal my sinkers and rods.

They had bad hygiene, they slept in cars not hotel rooms. They were racists. And they were all, without exception, experts on fishery management, and did not believe in conservation. "Let me tell youse something," one of these Neanderthals might say, "there are still plenty of fish out there just off shore somewhere, we don't need regulations." They used prostitutes. With that said, they were lovable and my clients. I did not like when they were on other boats. They knew to show up on time and to not talk to any other boats about where we fished.

I became a good fisherman quickly because many of my customers were Greek, they were never impressed—they wanted meat and their coolers overflowing. Anything short of triple the limits was a failure. Many of them worked in the garment industry in NYC, so they stopped coming when white rich people stopped buying fur completely.

I would never allow any drugs or booze on the boat. If you so much as cracked a beer I would turn around and say, "listen I'm happy to take you on a booze cruise but we will leave the rods at the dock. I fished at night and it could be dangerous." Alcohol brings ambition and suppresses motor skills. And the pills…the pills people had with them were their artificial self-assurance, and they brought an aloofness about them that everything was going to be ok. I used to get incensed. I'd yell at people, "Why take drugs? Look at this, look how beautiful this all is, the sun set and the sun rise. Look at the fish, why, it can't get better." Sadly, years later I became a hypocrite—I had 28 years sober at one time, when I started drinking with a woman. But more about that later.

One thing in common with all diehard striped bass fisherman, or at least an observation I like to register, is they don't get laid. That is, they don't pull no pussy. They're bad with women. Why else would they be out on a fucking boat on Saturday night with me?

I know this because I was one of them… I got lucky a few times in college and high school with hot chicks (play along) but then I had one too many bad acid trips, and I got nervous around women. I could not talk. I also came quick. That is, I was a first rate premature ejaculator, not good for repeat business. I could not delay satisfaction, even to this day. At a grocery store I start eating shit as I'm walking through the store…once I ate an entire roasted chicken and threw the carcass up in the shelves, then walked up to the cashier, with the wrapper, and grease all over me and sheepishly said, "Sorry I could not wait."

In the name of candor, I went 5 years once without getting laid (the strive for five), then I got a hand job from an old high school girlfriend; it was great and kept me from killing anyone (I'm convinced that all mass murderers are not getting laid). But it was not enough to build momentum. So I went another five pussy-less years. I spent a lot of time sitting in shitty smoke filled AA basements, with mostly older men (there were no hot chicks in AA meetings in the late 80s). Though I must admit I had a chance with a real drunk slob after a comedy show in New York, around four and a half years in, and I did not want to break the streak. The strive for five.

Chapter 4

The reality of being on the sea

During my 10 years as a charter boat captain in Montauk NY I issued five Maydays... all with horrified paying customers on board, many of which I lured in through Groupon.

In all five cases the boats were sinking and we were in danger. I never called the Coast Guard unless we were in imminent danger for our lives; if my boat simply broke down under normal circumstances I would call towing services like Sea Tow or Boat US, I subscribe to both, or have a friend tow me in. I have also been trapped on a little boat by myself in 40 mph sustained winds and pelting rain, and did not call the Coast Guard because I did not want any of them to get hurt or be out in lightning. I'd rather die than put a kid in danger. I don't want to bother anyone.

The level of danger I put paying customers in ranged from swamped boats to outright sinking, with customers in the water swimming for shore.

There was only one marginal circumstance where I probably did not need to call the Coast Guard but did. We could have made it through the night, and Seatow could have gotten us the next day. On a scale to one to ten it was a 5. (A 1 being running out of gas at night and calling the Coast Guard to tow you in because you were cold— note I never had a one, and I don't think they would come for that anyway.) But in this case I blew a belt on the water pump and could not fix it in time, nor could I get the anchor out due to a tangle in the Anchor compartment.(disorder /negligence, no redundancy) So, with no power we went through a bunch of rip tides, conspicuous rough water areas where the depth changes abruptly from approximately 50 feet to 25, causing big waves that in bad conditions could and have swamped boats. The "rips" are where the striped bass like to feed on disoriented and stunned bait fish. That is where we want to put our lures. When there's a full moon, which is when this customer specifically chose to fish—he booked that date six months in advance, and drove from South Jersey to catch a slob striped bass with me—the rip is more pronounced than usual as the tide is stronger. It steadily builds as the tide strengthens. In the middle of the tide there can be seven feet of breaking waves, especially if there's wind against tide. All waves are caused by wind.

To make matters worse we were fishing on an outgoing tide, with a hard southwest wind causing the waves to stand up like a surfing movie. We were drifting backwards in a precarious old beat up 1974 Bertram. A Bertram is one of those deep V boats and ironically one of the most popular charter trolling boats in the world. It is probably the worst drifting boat ever made. And god help you if you break down in high seas.

Anyone that has been out on a calm day and hit by the wake of a passing boat knows that when you're hit by a big wake from another boat you will be uncomfortable. You must brace for impact. You will rock back and forth when the wake hits you for a couple of seconds. You may pump your fist at the offending boat, expressing your indignation, or try to raise him on a VHS radio and call to tell him to slow down. Possibly including some vulgarity. And then you go on your way, no harm done.

It's different in a Bertram, though. What happens with the Bertram is that the wake hits the boat, but after a minute, rather than subside like a normal boat, it gains momentum. This is not just me and the Bertram I happened to buy. I did not have a defective model. It's every Bertram, ask any owner and they will tell you this, that's why they're always on the market. A wave hits it and takes on a force of its own, like some horrific carnival ride, operated by a deranged ex-con, pushing the lever to high speed, like they used to do at Action Park in Jersey (they finally closed due to many deaths and lawsuits). A small wave hits the idle fucking Bertram, and the boat will start to thrust back and forth. This phenomena is known as the "death rocks," where a boat rocks from left to right so violently that it forces everyone to hold on. And they hear everything in the cabin getting smashed about. Even on a calm day, a small wake from a passing boat will send everything flying in the cabin.

Beautiful, magnificent in design and style, particularly the 25 foot "Moppie," it is a visual work of art. I feel bad when speaking poorly of this classic, after all, who am I to speak of boat design...

But back to this particular excursion it was to be a quick local evening twilight trip. I prefer the incoming tides as there are fewer waves and less swell, as well as a calmer drift as the predominant south west wind runs with the tide, serving to keep the waves down. But this customer's schedule did not accommodate a calm trip.

We had to deal with the outgoing tide and six foot swells, and down one engine we trolled a wire line that sinks quick. We had to get our bait and an umbrella rig, (a bunch of lures on a bar that resembles a school of bait fish) down to the fish. The customer, my client, probably about 50 or maybe 55, had read my previous book, *Caught*, about striped bass addiction and selling fish on the black market. He was a fan and, again, a real genuine nice guy. I really wanted him to catch. I had made a deal for him: $300 for 4 hours. I would make money on this trip because I was only running one engine and would burn at most 5 gallons, even on a hard full moon tide.

The tide was screaming. Even with no wind the outgoing tide in the "rips" of Montauk point can produce 6 footers 3 seconds apart. Add in the predominant summer south west wind against the moon tide at even seven knots and you'll get some eight footers on the high spots and ledges where the big fish hide, waiting to ambush their pray. Some waves even break just as if you were on the beach, where the water goes from 45 feet to 20. The Elbow, Endeavor Shoals, and Shagwong Rips are known for this.

I was pushing the boat hard to move against the strong tide. Wire line is not hard to work with but it takes some nuance, like all fishing. Anyone can do it but one has to develop a feel. But in this case, on this night, the customer had little experience with trolling wire, and I had no mate to help him, and I was up in the bridge. I had never had a boat with a bridge before. I was too far from the customer. As I didn't have a mate I needed to work closely with them. The customer was letting the wire line out too fast and it was tangling or bird nesting on the reel. I only had one rod left so I instructed him to climb up to the bridge and drive the boat. This was no easy feat as there was no ladder, but he made it up. He was into it! We were in this together.

There's a murphy's law that if you let a customer drive the boat, no matter how innocuous the circumstance seems, no matter how much experience the customer has, it always seems to end problematically. God forbid there's one lobster pot in the vicinity. Because the customer seems to always aim directly for that pot, often hitting it and getting rope caught in the prop. If there's one boat 5 miles from where you handed over the helm, somehow you will come within inches of hitting it. You show the customer a heading on compass, and they say they have it. Trust me, they don't have it. You look up and you're doing

360s, like something out of the *Blair Witch Project*. Point is: never let the customer drive the boat.

*

If I may digress for a moment to illustrate this point, I had a group come out from Flushing, Queens one day for an afternoon trip. This was a while later as I was already using Groupon, where they'd purchased this trip. They were a nice young group, excited about a fun day of fishing.

We were only going six knots out the inlet and there were no boats in front of us or behind, so I asked one of the young ladies if she could drive for a second. She declared loudly: "Me!" Everyone gave the obligatory laughter, but I got her in the seat and told her to just go straight out the inlet, which was firmly flanked by two large conspicuous rocky jetties with people fishing on them. I did not even need to point out that there was nowhere else to go but out the inlet, into the ocean were we were going to fish. It's funny, she was young, probably 18, but I remember my thinking on this: as she was from Flushing there was a chance she did not know how to drive a car, but I assumed she had played video games. What 18 year old kid had not? Whether it be that game with skiers, or car games, the whole goal is to not hit the wall and crash. In this case the jetties with their huge rocks could only be viewed as walls or borders. Thus I was confident that she would not steer towards the wall and lose the game, especially in front of friends. This is really how I thought.

I ran back to where the rods were. I had untangled precisely one reel when I heard laughing. I looked up to find that she had inadvertently turned the boat toward jetties, and was about to crash into them. They were maybe 30 feet away, and even at 6 knots it would have caused damage and maybe hurt someone on the boat or the rocks. I grabbed the helm from her, threw the boat in reverse, missed the rocks by a couple feet, and then headed out the inlet, making a mental note to never again relinquish the wheel.

*

Back to my larger story, though. In this case, the guy was older, had his own boat, and we were in the open sea, and I simply needed him to steer the fucking boat. He willingly climbed up into the bridge as I let out the line below. The whole time I screamed to him over the wind and noise of engine how much throttle to use, so we could get the wire line out and umbrella rig down to the, hopefully, actively feeding striped bass. He was into it and so was I.

I had got most of the line out when I saw smoke coming from the engine compartment. I dropped the rod, and scurried up to the bridge. I looked at the temperature gauge and it read 3000, when it should have been 1400. Scared of melting the cylinder head, I shut her down. We were out of the rips and it was calm. In hind sight I should have thrown out the anchor and called Sea Tow or Boat US and discontinued the trip. Instead I tried to start the second engine that had a blown piston and an oil leak. I figured it could at least get us close to shore, and there I could figure out the anchor, but that engine did not start. I jumped back down into the cock pit. Now we were quickly moving adrift, powerless in a strong full moon tide, and headed right for the center of a very rough Polack rip with six foot waves. I opened the compartment, and saw that what I suspected had indeed happened: the water pump cooling belt had frayed and broken. I had a spare, but the engine was too hot, and the belt was not easy to get to. Just another experience of not being qualified to take people out for money.

I put the engine box back on just in time to brace for the impact of the boat hitting the rip. As expected, the boat rolled and listed violently from one side to the other as Bertrams do. I hit the deck and held on to the guard rail.

Then the next phase hit, the "death rocks." We were rocked side to side, like a ride at a low end carnival that had gone horrible wrong, unnaturally throwing people around like rag dolls.

I looked up to the bridge and saw that this poor, now hatless and drenched to the bone customer was being thrown about. The only thing keeping him on the boat was that his hands were locked on steering wheel.

Laterally, the top of the bridge would lean so far over that it would hit the water on the port side and then lunge back over and touch the water on the starboard side.

Eventually we passed through that rip and the boat steadied herself. I told the customer to come down from the bridge, but he was frozen in fear and did not move. I heard the next thunderous rip coming up on us—The Slot. I told him that we were approaching another rip and that if he could not make it down to the deck, he should lie down on the floor of the bridge as there he wouldn't take such a bad lashing. He did and held on to the base of what was once a ladder and deck rail. I gave him a life jacket and tied a 12 foot rope to it and then tied the rope to a cleat on the stern of the boat. I remember questioning my thinking on this. If the boat sank, I was pretty much attaching the customer to a giant anchor, assuring him a spot in Davey Jones' locker. I tried to let out the windless mechanical anchor but it was stuck. I had no time to crawl up to the bow as we were approaching The Slot, where 7 foot rollers awaited us.

And this time we were going backwards into the waves. We took on a lot water but most went through the scuppers and, critically, my bilge pumps were in working order.

We hit calmer waters, but I knew we had the Elbow, probably the worst rip, coming up. So I called the Coast Guard. I did not say mayday because we were not sinking but I said we were broken down, adrift and taking on water, which was true. After being thrown about like a cork, though, this guy deserved better. I did not care if they gave me a ticket or took the boat, this poor guy needed to get of this monstrosity.

We drifted out to sea in calm water for about five miles until the Coast Guard found us. I had a good flare. The Coast Guard tried to tow our hobbled craft back. They were friendly and professional. They were never condescending during rescues, always great guys. I recall that the poor customer was good natured and still tried to pay me for my efforts. Future customers in similar situations were not so accepting. Several tried suing me. The reality was that I was unprepared, should not have been doing a charter with one engine broken. I should have been skilled enough and had the tools to change the belt, had the common sense to drop the anchor and call Sea Tow and not bother the Coast Guard. They should only be called for dire emergencies.

Those calls were to come in spades that upcoming summer.

*

For 10 years, I ran part-time charters out of Montauk Harbor (on the easternmost tip of Long Island, New York, once dubbed the sport fishing capital of the world) off a small, 20 to

25 foot center console boat (a proud member of the Mosquito Fleet) with mediocre results, at best. My modest, if not entirely pathetic, charter fishing business was aptly named Second Choice Charters. The business had been dragging bottom and operating in the red with only 10 to 20 legitimate and documented trips a year. In lieu of real, paying customers, I'd mostly just take friends out for a spin. In the past, I considered a trip successful if the customers didn't stiff me or walk off with my rods and reels. But in 2017, to my utter shock, the business started flourishing. I was in high demand with more work than I could handle, thanks to one major online marketing and sales platform: Groupon.

The Groupon campaign worked amazingly well—too well, in fact. I quickly became one of the busiest boats in Montauk, sailing twice a day all week long. However, even though I was a licensed United States Coast Guard captain and my boat was a registered New York state charter boat, I was ill-equipped and grossly under-qualified for the job and workload, not to mention that the conditions on my boat were hardly pristine and not exactly seaworthy, with its ancient wiring, sporadic VHF, and small leaks in the transom, etc. Still, constantly driven by the allure of money, ego, and my distorted sense of entitlement, I pushed on.

The results were appalling over this two-year period. I had five Coast Guard rescues, all official Maydays, and three out-of-court cash settlements with disappointed and often horrified customers, which severely cut into my profit margin (not to mention losing the trip fare and tip for the day).

One settlement involved a 65-year-old Cuban/Canadian man. A real tool, if I may say so. He wore green camouflage running shorts and a matching tank top. After we disembarked, he changed into tight yoga pants. I remember he had a huge bulge and had no problem flaunting his well-endowed nature. Fishermen are all ballbusters, so I started in on him right away.

"Do you wear those to get women?" His friend laughed. He did not.

At 3 a.m., after a tremendous evening of bass fishing off Block Island, we ran out of gas within 200 yards of the inlet. It was a close call. We made it back 12 miles, but could not eke out the last of it on my old carbureted 250 Ocean Pro Evinrude outboard motor. So right in front of the Montauk inlet we sputtered and stalled. I immediately tried to throw the anchor, but thanks to my negligence and general untidiness, the anchor rope had gotten completely tangled with my chum pot line and some other stuff, rendering the anchor completely unusable. With the customers keenly watching me, and feeling as though I had to do something, I went through the motions. I threw the gnarled mess overboard, betting on the outside chance that it would remarkably and mysteriously untangle itself, perhaps through divine intervention. Alas, it only went down about 10 feet.

All the other boats that could have towed us in had docked already. We were a mile from the Coast Guard station and the Cuban/Canadian man was unwilling to say that he was in distress because of a health condition even though he had just completed a round of chemotherapy and had been complaining all night that his feet were cold and that he felt lightheaded. It was a stretch, but I would've had just cause to call the Coast Guard with a health concern. When I asked him if I could tell the Coast Guard about his condition, he turned nasty and growled, "Don't get me involved in your shit!" So instead, we drifted back out to sea with a hard, outgoing full moon tide and the wind against it.

After taking on heavy water while drifting, stern first, through the substantial five-foot rips, we were 10 miles offshore when the Coast Guard came to save us from our swamped vessel.

The final settlement was awarded to a terrorized father and son group from Lancaster, Pennsylvania, who purchased the Groupon voucher and came out for a nice day of fishing, only to end up frantically bailing out a flooded engine room assembly line style, with five-gallon buckets for two solid hours. Finally, the Coast Guard reluctantly came with their large high-power pumps. They emptied the water from the bilge and escorted us back to the harbor. The Coast Guard (all good guys) were sick of me by this point, and, with any less of an effort from the Lancaster boys, the intruding water would have covered the engine blocks and the boat would have surely sunk to the bottom of the sea.

*

When I first came to Montauk from Moriches, New York, I set out a green umbrella rig with 300 feet of wire. In what felt like no time at all, three 20-pound fish hit the deck; I was thrilled. I'd had some okay days bass fishing at Moriches, but nothing like this. I said to myself: "I will never leave this place they call the fishing Mecca. I will do anything it takes. I've got to do this; I have to fulfill my dream becoming a Montauk charter boat captain."

Mariners or wannabe captains, I encourage you to read on. I am confident that many of my stories are informative and funny; simply for the fact that no one got hurt, they are humorous cautionary tales.

Part Two

Chapter 5

Captain? I Should Never Have Been Out There or in Possession of Credentials

Yes, I was a *googan* (an endearing term for an amateur boater), a weekend warrior, a member of the Mosquito Fleet, but at least I wasn't one of those guys who added "captain" before my name, like doctors: "Captain" Jeff Nichols. I hear it all the time by wannabe captains. Anyone can take the three-week course, fudge a bunch of documents, get a certificate, and then go around calling themselves "captain," even if they'd spent the last 25 years as a middle school lunchroom supervisor. To put this in perspective, real water men like tugboat captains don't call themselves "captain."

Nor do I have my credentials proudly hanging on my office wall or above my fireplace like some charter boat captains are inclined to do. The USCG Operator of Uninspected Passenger Vessels (OUPV) License—commonly referred to as the "six-pack" or "Charter Boat Captain's License"—can take as little as three weeks to procure. The license now comes in the form of a passport, but it used to be like a diploma. It is the lowest of Coast Guard credentials, basically saying that you can be a guide. Admit it, you hack! You took a three-day course, some practice tests, and a four-hour exam. Plus, you lied about a bunch of sea time you don't really have.

No? Well, I guess I'm the only one.

I don't want to degrade the real charter boat captains who make a true living at fishing, day in and day out. It is a noble profession and very hard work; if done correctly, it is every bit as hard as commercial fishing. Montauk has a fine fleet of gorgeous, pristine, capable boats. That's why all these wannabes, these googans, are clamoring to get this credential: they feel that it somehow puts them in this respected occupation when, in reality, it does not.

Very few are suited for the charter fishing business. When I add up all the money I spent on boats, repairs, and dockage fees, it dwarfs any profit I made. Just to break even in the charter business with a 25-foot boat, you would need to do 30 charters per month. In other words, just having the certificate does not make you a charter boat captain.

Sure, the certificate looks official and serious with its obligatory formal wax stamp, wings, and pageantry. But, my god, who frames their six-pack captain's license and puts it on the wall? Someone who wants to brag and imply that they're a member of the Merchant Marines, perhaps? You may love the sea and fishing and be a damn good fisherman, but odds are you haven't done much on the sea, relatively speaking. I mean, you probably never skillfully navigated a barge full of civilian cargo through the Suez Canal during wartime, or negotiated a 100-ton barge under the Brooklyn Bridge, or sailed through the Strait of Magellan in South America, which my Gruncle Joshua Slocum actually did (a full chapter on this later). *NO*, you did not. You also didn't spend 20 years working on a commercial longliner. You took a 30-hour crash course and memorized a bunch of often outdated and redundant nautical terms, all of which you forgot as soon as you walked out of the test facility.

I mean, it's a free world; you can frame what you want. I talked to a car salesman in Riverhead who had his six-pack certification framed behind his desk at the dealership. It did look really nice, but it confused the hell out of me: *Are you captain or a car salesman?*

I guess what I'm saying is that most, if not all, six-pack "captains" are kind of posers.

Speaking of framed diplomas, the saddest thing I ever saw framed was when I was walking around the apartment of a girl I had just hooked up with (I know, can you imagine? A solid six, by the way). I knew she worked at a doctor's office, but she wasn't a nurse. As I surveyed her apartment, I saw that on her wall she had framed a Certificate to Draw Blood. That's what it said! "Blah blah blah *is vested by the State of New Jersey,* so blah blah blah is allowed to draw blood." This broke my heart and put me in a melancholy state. Like a CPR or first aid class, this certificate could not have taken more than a day to acquire. For some unknown reason, this poor woman felt the need to frame it and put it on her wall. It's like framing the sportsmanship award (which says, "You sucked, but you were nice when you were on the bench"). I think of Jack Nicholson in that marvelous movie, *About Schmidt,* in which older people struggling with identity and mediocrity end up with the framed "certificate of attendance" on the wall.

Most of us are modest when we get our captain's credentials, even a little bit sheepish, as we are aware that we are dipping our toe in a grand, historic profession.

I don't want to completely mitigate and discredit the achievement of obtaining a six-pack license; while it doesn't prove any aptitude for running an actual boat or taking care of a customer's safety, there is one section of the test—the chart plotting section—that is pretty rigorous and takes some practice, intelligence, and even some basic knowledge of algebra to pass it. You also have to know military time (you could have heard my two brain cells banging together to get this stuff down). I had always been confined to the learning disability classes throughout school, so I was choked up and very proud when I passed this section of the test. So now, I am being a hypocrite. Chart plotting is a cool craft that's not used much anymore thanks to GPS (just like we don't stop at gas stations for directions anymore). So, passing this portion of the test shows you are, indeed, capable of some seamanship, which is no small feat. Hell, where is my certificate? I'm going to frame it and stick it on my damn wall after all.

I guess it's just a pet peeve of mine. I heard one weekend warrior on the docks who owned a 22-foot Pro-Line (a modest boat, yet you always need help docking it), who had just gotten his six-pack license the week before. He probably had zero charters under his belt and definitely did not have the sea time to be a captain, but there he was, regaling a small group of people who were trying to take in a nice sunset. In a dead serious tone, he told them that, according to "nautical law," he had the authority to marry a couple at sea. Can you believe the gall of that guy? Basically it is not legit for even a Navy captain to marry someone. So, don't let a captain talk you into marriage.

By the way, this same person had his name stenciled onto the side of his truck—"Blah Blah Charters, Montauk"—with a gorgeous mermaid and a hook. What's worse is that he had the same name as a famous eyeglass company. Eventually, he had to remove the sign from his truck's door and just put "Captain Joe" there instead.

Not only do I not refer to myself as "Captain Jeff" (my voicemail does not say, "Hi, you've reached Captain Jeff of *Second Choice Charters*"), I also never even told anyone I had passed the test until a year later. I was honestly ashamed that I still had problems docking a 25-foot boat into a slip during a mild wind. I banged into other boats all the time, so how could I go around telling people I'm a sea captain?

After 15 year of fishing, spending six months of each year on the water, six 18-hour days a week, I am still embarrassed to tell people I'm a captain. I like to think of myself as a competent guide and gentleman fisherman who smells sometimes.

When I'm around real sea folk, people who make an actual living at sea, I am always very impressed and interested in what they do. If I meet them at a party or the gym or happen to sit next to them on an airplane, whether they're commercial fisherman, tugboat captains, Navy personnel, ferry pilots, or oil rig workers, I always hope they don't ask me what I do for a living, and if they do, I tell them I'm a substitute teacher and enjoy playing golf.

In the same breath, I also wilt when my mother proclaims triumphantly that I am an author: "My son's an author!" Can you imagine the collective eye-rolling at the country club when she announces this? (She is a member of a country club that James Patterson and other famous authors often frequent.)

I'm not an author. I am a funny motherfucker, a humorist that can tell a story, who is capable of banging out an occasionally amusing article from time to time, for which I get paid (like my notable letter to the editor of *Teen Beat* magazine, for instance).

I am not without some writing prowess, and I've had a few accomplishments in the literary field. So, calling me a writer would be fine, but calling me an "author" demeans the profession. There was a point in recent history, before Facebook made us all "writers," that being an author was considered an esteemed profession. When, say, Jack London, Norman Mailer, or John Irving used to walk into a room, people would shake in their boots, and they should have. These people were rock stars, capable of doing what others could not with language through metaphor, detail, and suspense, and since the work in creating a cohesive and entertaining novel is so difficult to achieve, they

49

deserve all the accolades they can get. Literature was regarded as the highest of art forms, on a par with painting. In fact, I believe writing fiction is the hardest thing in the world to do, with keeping the reader interested, working on micro and macro levels, adding recurring characters and themes. When you start reading a Charles Dickens or Jonathan Franzen, you know instantly that you're in the hands of a master craftsman.

Point is, when I die, please don't say I was a captain or an author. Just write something like this on my tombstone:

Here lies Jeff Nichols . . .

A witty fellow.

He fished some, wrote some,

but mostly ate a lot of junk food and napped.

Or the obituary could read: *Jeff Nichols was a nice guy that liked to laugh and drew immense pleasure from his friends (all three of them). He was a writing and fishing enthusiast. He was disorderly, often smelled bad, and never had a real occupation. He also lost his keys a lot. Sometimes, he would find them, but then lose them again. As his friend Dan playfully observed, "Jeff overcame very little to accomplish nothing."*

Like I said earlier, I have made some money on my own, including my first book, *Trainwreck: My Life as an Idiot*, which Simon & Schuster published in 2009. It was later made into a movie, *American Loser*, which became an HBO feature presentation. All told (including speaker fees), I made over $200,000 there—not a future, but better than the proverbial stick in the eye. It was a nice feeling of accomplishment to get those checks, but in the end, it all went right back into the disease that is fishing: bigger boats, better rods, electronics, etc.

***

Anyway, back to the test. I took the test because, like a lot of us, I had a lifelong dream of becoming a charter boat captain. I was bit by the charter fishing bug early.

Years later, my friends and I chartered a boat out of Montauk. We all had shitty entry-level jobs, and I remember being mesmerized by the captain when he told me they were going for tuna the next day. I remember asking him, "You get to go tomorrow, too?" I couldn't fathom a cooler job in the world (little did I know). Whoever wrote that book, *Do What You Love, The Money Will Follow*, should be beaten with a stick.

Acquiring a six pack is a modest first step to becoming a captain, but there is a lot more to it. Another step is getting a job working on the water in some capacity for an extended amount of time. How long? Certainly more than being a mate for six weeks on a party boat, but that does help. Every day you're on the water helps. But being behind the helm in various sea conditions is the most critical step, and the majority of new captains with six-packs just don't have this experience—including myself when I first got my six-pack. I have it now, god knows. I've seen a lot shit and learned from a lot of mistakes. The only good news is that nobody died.

Chapter 6

How To Pass The Exam

Make no mistake, I have a valid captain credential. I don't want to mitigate the exam; the test itself is hard. There's a lot of material to cover: safety equipment, antiquated nautical law, chart plotting, fishing rules, etc. No matter how smart you are, if you don't study, you won't pass. Likewise, if you are of average intelligence, then study your ass off and you will pass. Sea schools now offer three-day crash courses and practice tests on the computer. If you do these practice tests repetitively, you'll eventually recognize the answers, even if you don't know what they really mean.

But all that information you will have memorized, including the obsolete nautical terms, will be wiped from your brain the moment you walk out of the testing site. A Harvard grad who was on the sailing team might feel like he could simply walk in and pass the test, but he wouldn't know that no one passes that test without relentlessly studying. It serves as a great equalizer in that regard; a plumber can become a captain if he studies hard enough. Still, the test's major flaw is that it's entirely academic. Other than the chart plotting section, which constitutes a quarter of the test and demands actual motor skills using a compass, ruler, some light Algebra, and adding military time, there is no obligation to prove any practical application of the material. In other words, there is no "road test," which is a major problem.

Case in point: A woman once worked as a chef on a cruise line, and her boyfriend, who was studying for the test, convinced her to take the test with him. She was smart and studied hard, and, despite having never driven so much as a Boston Whaler, she passed the written test. And since she was able to claim sea time from working on a ship, she technically had all of the hours she needed, and her senior officer signed off on them. You could be in a coma on a boat, and your hours will count as sea time; that's a problem! She passed the physical and was already in a mandatory drug testing program, so she got her six pack captain credential like 10,000 other bozos (myself included) have. But she didn't stop there. Aptly, she liked to acquire credentials, so she sat for the next licenses, all the way up the 100-ton boat captain's license; she passed that, too. Now, this woman is legally qualified to drive a small passenger ferry, even though she'd never spent 10 minutes on the bridge of a boat. Scary!

Do we see the problem here?

*

Once I got my license, I didn't want to piss off the established local charter boats, so I hung what I thought was a benign, inauspicious shingle in front of a pylon by the slip were I kept my boat that read, "Second Choice Charters," with the tagline: "If the top boats can't take you, I will."

I was doing okay with the small (21 to 26 feet) outboard engine boats, but I was clearly in over my head when I moved up to a 31-foot Bertram with only one running diesel engine. The few people at the time who could help me with maintenance and mechanical work had left Montauk for various reasons (one moved to North Carolina to become a crabber; others simply got sick of me asking for help).

By 2016, I was completely alone, and anyone who knows can tell you it is very hard to find any kind of professional mechanic in Montauk. And then, trying to find a diesel mechanic in Montauk? You can forget about it. There's one guy, but he works almost exclusively on Cummings. There are 11,000 boats in Montauk harbor, but the marinas can't hire help because the cost of housing is so high—a condo can cost $10K a month in the summer.

The differences between an outboard engine, which is largely self-contained, and twin inboard engines with a shaft are dramatic. In short, a lot more shit can go wrong on an inboard than an outboard.

The truly scary part is that the inboard engines are cooled largely by seawater that's pumped into the boats using Imperials, which are known to break and seize. Now, the hulls have holes from which the hoses draw sea water to cool the engines. There's a lot that can go wrong with this kind of cooling system. The hoses can dry out and crack, and they can also separate from their brackets. The clamps and pumps can break. The belts can fall off and require constant inspection. One or any combination of these issues can cause massive seawater intrusion into the bilge (roughly 100 gallons per minute, which adds up to 1,000 gallons in just 10 minutes) and quickly sink the boat.

Also, there's a lot of gear behind the keel of the boat that outboard powered boats don't have, like rudders and shafts. All of these are bolted into the hull. If you hit a submerged object, like a rock or log, with the prop or shaft, it can rip that stuff off, causing the whole boat to sink due to massive water intrusion.

A responsible captain can temporarily fix these issues, allowing the boat to make it safely home. A good captain should be so attuned to his craft that he recognizes an extra five gallons in his boat. Now, obviously, he can't control catastrophic engine failure or a tranny blowing, and no amount of tools will help him with this at sea. But the captain will need to be able to fix the basics (e.g., a blown hose, clogged fuel pump, a belt popping off, etc.) if he wants to be a genuine Montauk charter boat captain.

*

After 20 years of operating (not just sleeping on) a sport fishing boat, I'd have hoped, by now, I knew something about basic water and passenger safety such as:

- How to operate flares and fire extinguishers
- Have a solid command of anchoring techniques (when to anchor for safety and recreation, how much line to use depending on depth and tide, etc.)How to operate and interpret radar
- How to run a boat in the fog with a compass
- How to radio in coordinates from GPS to the Coast Guard
- Knowing all the boating rules, including a general understanding of buoys (what red and green mean) and using lights at night
- Familiarity with general boat maintenance

However, when I got my legitimate charter boat captain credential in 2002, I knew basically nothing about how to operate a boat or about passenger safety. For instance, I didn't know what a type IV floating device was, and I certainly didn't have one. Miraculously, thank god, in my early years, no one got hurt or drowned. As I often fish at night in rough seas, this could have happened easily, especially at night while fishing rips under a full moon.

When my friend, Craig Hase, and I first started, we thought that the big stripers were staged in the strongest part of a rip (that's not true). We would head to the heart of the growing rip lines (we did not know that waves built when the tide rises), where the water went from 40 to 18 feet, causing, when the wind was against the tide, crashing seven-foot waves.

Chapter 7

You Don't Need a Gorgeous Boat to Charter

In the charter business, you don't necessarily need a 35-foot custom BMH, Osmond, Viking, or Yellowfin. You can run a very good business with many satisfied customers on a boat that is not aesthetically pleasing at all. Case in point: The charter boat, *Obsession*, run by Rodger Brevet out of Montauk, was not exactly easy on the eyes. It was a General Marine used primarily as a charter boat for 30 years. Brevet also had 30 years of night commercial fishing under his belt on this craft. It's hard to imagine that it ever looked nice, even when new. The boat was long, narrow, and rough around the edges. It looked slightly tired, like the boat in the classic movie, *The African Queen*, with Humphrey Bogart and Katharine Hepburn. Brevet kept busy into the 1990s and sailed all the time. No matter how reluctant people were to board at first, nine times out of 10, they returned happy.

For years, Brevet had a steady customer base not because he had a great boat, but because he could bend the rods and catch fish as well as anyone. In fact, the nicest boats in the Montauk fleet would often anchor up next to Brevet, hoping to get in on the action, and then they'd have to leave after watching Brevet's customers laughing and exchanging high fives, while their own customers on their "nicer" boats sat fishless and quiet. If you want to get into this business, you have to realize one basic rule: No fish means miserable customers, no matter how nice your boat is.

Brevet succeeded because he was funny and good with people, in a gruff kind of way, but also because he was mechanically inclined. These three common themes are crucial for running a successful charter boat:

1. Preventative maintenance
2. Resourceful spending
3. Being organized

After that comes fishing ability and passion.

While you don't need a great boat, you do need a safe boat. I did not have that.

A trip I took to Quepos, Costa Rica, on the Pacific coast, confirmed my belief that a flashy boat was not necessary for a great charter business. Back in 2000, I went on the trip with a bunch of high rollers in the construction business. I didn't know most of the guys, and I wound up with them because of a friend of a friend. Somehow, the lead guy's secretary booked the wrong boat. The guy had wanted to go out on a gorgeous 42-foot Viking, but something fell through, and when we got to the dock that morning, the boat we thought we had booked already had people on it. Despite the ensuing obligatory barrages of texts and phone calls, power moves, and flat-out yelling, nothing could be done about it. Since all the other nice boats were already taken, we walked down the docks in search of anything seaworthy. The high roller was furious and ready to spend big, but Costa Rica, at least where we were staying, had a limited number of high performance luxury fishing vessels, most of which are run by seasonal American captains.

We were about to give up when I noticed a small boat at the end of the dock with two men waving me over, obviously encouraging me to check out their operation. To say the vessel gave an underwhelming first impression is an understatement. The boat was tired. It wasn't even a Bertram, which were common there because they were good trolling boats. It was, instead, an old Chris-Craft with worn, sun-bleached paint. Its deck had clearly never been treated with a gelcoat or bottom finish, and it also looked soft, like a boat you would see on someone's lawn with a cardboard sign saying, "FREE." Or on Craigslist: "Engine needs some work, but . . ."

What caught my eye was the open cooler, which was filled with bloody ice and had a steady red stream draining down the scuppers. I remembered the same bloody ice on Rodger Brevet's boat, and he was the best in the business. It also smelled of diesel fuel and looked like Brevet's boat. They must have been commercial fishing the night before because they opened up another cooler that had a bunch of mahi-mahi (a.k.a. dorado), which they were unloading into boxes. The fish were gorgeous, some probably 15 to 20 pounds. The rods looked old, but their lines looked new and functional. They also had nice, well-maintained green spreader bars. So, the gaffs, bloody ice, and deck were all painting a good picture of a capable and productive fishing boat.

They offered to take us out for $300 dollars. Interested, I waved at the high roller, telling him to come over. I asked the fishermen how they did the day before; they told me they'd had an excellent catch: three marlin, some sailfish, and a bunch of yellowfin. I grabbed my new fat cat friend, who was reluctantly approaching, and pulled him to the boat. "Let's go catch."

After a superficial glance, he was repulsed and angry, proclaiming, "I wouldn't get on that thing if the land was on fire." He walked back down the dock, huffing and puffing. Apparently, he spent the rest of the day drinking and hanging with what looked like an underage prostitute—all I know is he got into a lot trouble with the hotel and local authorities. I looked at another guy with me and asked, "Wanna go and split it?" He said sure, and away we went.

The day was calm and magnificent. The Ecuadorian men were polite, sincere, and eager to catch with us.

And catch we did! On the way out, close to the rocks on the shore, we landed a roosterfish, which we released, and then a snook that we kept and ate that night; the hotel restaurant cooked it for us.

Then, after some trolling around, we had probably landed six sailfish, totaling 100 pounds. Exhilarated, we switched over our bait to try to land a more edible fish than the sailfish. The captain noticed some dolphins were swimming nearby, and we trolled around them. We got no hits, so the guy changed bait; he put a ballyhoo on and hooked a 250-pound blue marlin almost instantly, which the crew kept (I assume to sell—I wish they had not). Then, they put spreader bars out and landed five small yellowfin tuna, totaling 50 pounds. Basically, we caught so many fish we almost sank the boat. It was a tremendous outing while the fat cat was dealing with the authorities at the hotel pool (underage prostitution is a sad and despicable problem in Costa Rica and other fishing destinations; fortunately, Costa Rica has cracked down hard on it).

Not only did we have blast, but we also had a safe time catching fish, and we weren't even on a custom 42-foot Viking.

That operation convinced me that it's possible to run great, productive, safe trips on small, old, unimpressive boats. However, it was not as easy as it looked. The crew was resourceful, and they were good mechanics. They must have taken their tough old engine apart and put it back together many times, they had to have been sharp and known how to improvise solutions, probably going to junk yards to replace parts. Frugal and cagey, that crew proved that a gorgeous boat can never replace a capable charter crew.

Chapter 8

The Bertram From Hell

Whether it's buying a car, house, or boat, there are often moments in hindsight when you know you should have walked away but did not.

In January 2017, when the many Groupon orders were rolling in, I knew it was time to dump the 33-foot Hydra Sport Vector, as the soggy, water-laden hull and big twin 250-horsepower engines simply burned too much gas. It was time to make the transition to a single-screw diesel and burn five gallons per four-hour trip rather than 60-plus gallons on the Vector. I thought I'd finally make some money fishing.

In the middle of February, it's tough to find a boat in the water to test drive. I had $20k to spend, after dumping the Vector for the insanely low price of $8,500 to a friend—with two new lower units and one new power head, I might add. This was not the only boat I had taken a bath on. There were many seasons I owed the marina money; I had no money for storage or winterizing and storing boats, so I would sell them for whatever price I could get: not much.

I looked at a boat in East Hampton called the *Even Keel*. It was perfect for me: an old (1979), weathered, 31-foot Blue Hill

Mariner (BHM) lobster boat with a Caterpillar natural and diesel gas engine. I brought a mechanic friend along to meet the owner, a retired East Hampton commercial fisherman who had great maintenance records and, you could tell, had taken good care of her. I remember he documented his oil changes in pencil near the helm. The guy was meticulous, as one has to be to run a business.

We ran a hose to the engine and fired it up. It sounded good, but my friend said the old Cat looked like it belonged in a museum taking a nap in a World War II truck. The thing was almost 40 years old, so she couldn't have much life left, he suspected. According to Caterpillar, 8,000 hours equals about 3/4 of its life.

The owner, very likable, wanted $30k. It was in good shape, had nice electronics, but he was trying to get too much, I felt. I offered $19k. He did not bite, but rumor has it that he took less than that when the summer came.

I kept looking online, mostly on the nationwide Facebook group, Fisherman's Garage Sale. I found a Topaz on there that I thought might work, though it was twin screw, with twin Yanmar diesels that had 2,000 hours on them. The ad said that the boat was a little beat up—perfect for me!—and had good electronics. It was listed at $17.5k.

I called, and the owner said the boat was available. But he was in Florida and would not be back in New Jersey, where the boat was, for another three weeks. This would have been okay—I normally had no problem waiting—but I was dating a new girl who was a little out of my league, and I was spending money like a drunken prize fighter to impress her: trips to NYC and Florida, concerts, and lot of dinners out. In fact, I may as well have been a drunken prize fighter—I had begun drinking with this woman after having no alcohol touch my lips in 29 years! I also smoked pot with her. I must admit, we did have fun. Booze was made for dating—a marvelous social lubricant. I drank a few more times after the girl and I broke up, but I've been on the wagon ever since. I don't want to make light of this. In the end, better not to drink if you can, if only because you get away with more shit when you're sober. As I mentioned before, I have seen good fisherman crash and burn because of booze. If I drank in my forties, I would have never become the angler I am today.

Anyway, the problem was that my $20,000 boat budget was now down to $15,000 and was rapidly declining. And the guy from Jersey with the Topaz, which would been ideal for me, did not want to hear my $15k offer. I called the guy a week later; he was nice about it, but he told me not to bother coming, as someone was coming with the $17k that weekend. Coincidentally (and maddeningly), the person who bought it drove it back to Montauk, as well, with no issues, and it is presently docked at the Montauk Marine Basin.

I went to Craigslist with a realistic budget of $14k. There was a boat I had my eye on for a while (by the way, buying boats is a disease in and of itself and can ruin many a marriage): a 1974 28-foot diesel Bertram.

*

I had always liked the look of Bertrams, mostly the 25-foot Mojo with its clear windows, indoor tables inside, and the lamp (they look so neat and classy at night with light on). They're good trolling boats, used all over the world for mahi-mahi and sailfish and tuna.

I knew, from working with Jimmy George, how to troll wire line for bass, so that's what I would do; I'd also envisioned trolling for yellowfin at the canyon. Bertrams are also good in a head sea, so no worries making it out in a storm. On the other hand, they're also designed with the Ray Hunt standard 24-degree deadrise deep-V hulls, and they were infamously terrible for drift fishing and getting caught in the rips around Montauk, which is exactly what I would be doing. Deep Vs rock severely while drifting in the slightest of chops or wakes, causing things to fly around the deck and cabin and, worst of all, causing seasickness. My previous boat (the Vector) was a deep V, too, and rocked a lot on the drift. But the Bertrams, because they are top heavy with a bridge, are in a class by themselves as far as "death rocks" go. And thus, the puking passengers.

But I felt if I bumped it up on the drift and took her in and out of gear, I could keep her from rocking. And despite not knowing how to do basic maintenance on them, I liked the idea of twin diesels, so who cared if they were off brand Isuzus?

Everyone told me to stay away from this boat. On top of every other problem it had, I'd find out later that the only diesel mechanic in Montauk only works on Cummins and Yamahas, nothing else—that's all they want in Montauk. So, of course, I headed toward Brooklyn in early February to check out this boat.

People also warned me against buying in Brooklyn. The marina is right off the Belt Parkway, so there was a chance that Hurricane Sandy had damaged it. Even if it hadn't been damaged by the hurricane, you simply don't buy a boat in fucking Brooklyn! . . . as a rule, that is. But I'd had a good experience with a small boat I bought in Sheepshead Bay, a 17-foot VIP with a newer 115 Yamaha four-stroke. A great little boat. I'd gotten it for $5k and managed to put on 600 flawless hours on her in two seasons before I sold it for $4k.

So, Brooklyn did not scare me.

It was the middle of February when I went to meet the guy; I did not bring a mechanic the first time. The boat yard was unimpressive, a dark, forlorn place. A real shithole. It's hard to believe that it could be nice even in nicer weather. There were a lot shitty, off-brand boats: Trophy boats, Bayliners, and old dilapidated Chris Crafts. None of them shrink wrapped. A lot of sailboats, some had clearly been abandoned years ago and were rotting away.

I found the guy right away—Joey. He was Spanish or Puerto Rican and nice enough. He told me he was the head mechanic of the boat yard (I would later find out this was only partially true; the marina had no onsite staff) and lead me to the Bertram.

So far, so good.

The boat looked okay. Joey had water going to the engines via a hose, and he cranked them over for me. I took video and sent it to my mechanic friend, who said that the diesels sounded good.

By the way, after you buy a piece of shit, friends come out of the woodwork just to say, "You should've had me come and look at it with you—I would've told you not to buy it." But when you ask them to come check out a boat with you, they're never around, or at a funeral, or their kid's sick, or something else comes up. Still, when they see the boat, they start in with that "you should have called me" shit. While I've had a lot of fun and bonded with a lot of people in Montauk, I never had consistent, reliable friends in the 18 years I've been fishing out here. There is so much ego involved with fishing, and this can alienate people. Also, many of the people I fished hard with, sadly, got hooked on oxycodone, moved away, or got old and died. It's critical to have reliable friends in the charter boat fishing business, someone who sticks by you all the time and knows their shit. Jimmy George was that guy for me, but he left town.

Joey happened to be a diesel mechanic for the City of NY—that's where he got the Isuzu engines, from the city box trucks. This isn't necessarily a deal breaker because all diesel engines are ubiquitous (even in Cummins, which are the same ones in the trucks, only they've been marinized, given special paint and a cooling system). He worked at the marina occasionally on weekends. He was a fast talker but seemed to know his shit, and he was really into the boat.

Joey had marinized the engines himself. He was very convincing and confident in the boat. He called it his "baby" and project boat, explaining the cooling system and tranny and how much time he'd spent putting in all the different features (the new canvas, for example, cost him $1,000 bucks). All this was true, and you could tell the guy put in a lot work and spent a lot of money on the boat: brand new engine hatch covers, new starters and alternators, the wiring was all new, a working head, a new refrigerator, A/C, and blue LED deck lighting. The fact that Joey had put his name on the back of the boat, the *JoeyL*, spoke volumes to the amount of time, energy, and cash he'd put into making it his dream boat. The boat was not designed for the diesel engines, yet he'd fit them into a tight spot and got them running, which was some feat in and of itself. You had to tip your hat to that effort.

But still, why was he selling it? And why had it not sold yet? The reason he'd told me he was selling—"Kid's gotten too big, so it was time to sell and move up"—did not ring true for some reason. Looking back, that was just one of the many red flags I should've been paying attention to.

Joey had spent so much money putting these engines into the boat, to simply abandon it after only two years, and at such a low price, seemed suspicious. On top of this, he was only moving up two feet to a 30-foot Pursuit Tierra and putting new Volvo engines in them. I was familiar with the old Pursuit Tierra—yes, it is roomier, but not much. If he'd said he was getting rid of it because the engines were too old or the boat rocked too much, it would've been more believable. His moving up shtick probably scared away some more prudent buyers. But not me. Even with all these red flags, I was interested. I should've walked right then.

Instead, I made what I thought was a lowball offer of $13k, pending sea trial. He said 14k. I said fine.

Since he was a mechanic, I asked if I could pay him extra to get me in running shape for the long steam back to Montauk. He told me he'd clean it up good, do an oil change, replace the oil filters and impellers and water pump, and have it running great. He said he'd also change the internal fuel filters, too. It all sounded great.

But then, I explained that I needed all this done because I was going to drive it 120 miles back to Montauk. He bridled at this—a third red flag: "120 miles? That's too far. You should have it trailered" (to this day, I'm convinced that Joey doesn't really know where Montauk is). "Why?" I said, "They're diesel engines; they're designed for long halls." His answer should have been, "Smart idea! If you have the time, that's the way to go." Another walk away moment I should've taken—gone.

I gave him a $1,000 deposit, agreeing to pay the remainder of the agreed upon price only if the test drive was successful and he'd actually changed the fuel filters, gotten the inside steering working, changed the oil, and fixed the radar—all of which had been per our agreement.

Then came the barrage of bullshit. You should've heard this guy talk. On top of all the other changes he'd said he'd do, Joey ran his mouth about how he gets the Isuzu "parts" at half price and would have the boat in great running shape. And if I had any problems once I got it to Montauk, he'd personally drive out there to help me. And I believed him. (Boy, my blood is boiling just thinking about it now.) I think, on some level, he meant it, but it was unrealistic (for him at least). He needed time to work on his new boat. Also, it was snowing every week in late February early March, and he needed his job and family more than he needed the extra two grand. It was clear that he was also hiding something. (I wouldn't want to see this guy walking down the street as I waited in my car at a red light. I'd run him over.)

Next was the test drive, which we scheduled for two weeks later. When the day arrived, I drove all the way to Brooklyn from Montauk again. But when I got there, the boat was boxed in by a dumpster; we couldn't get past it, so we couldn't test drive the boat. Joey had been there for two hours; he could have easily called and told me to turn around. He did not. So, I drove back to Montauk—three hours.

The following week I drove back, and for $300 they dropped the boat in the water (most marinas in Montauk charge $3 a foot, so $150 would have been a fair price).

Next, I found a mechanic on Craigslist who normally charged $500 for a survey, but since I was close to Oceanside, where he lived, he would "look at it" for $250. He was an hour and half late, citing the "awful Belt traffic." And he had no tools. (By the way, what's the deal with mechanics having no tools? I'm always surprised when mechanics show up empty-handed, and it happens a lot. That'd be like a sea tow guy showing up with no rope or a barber with no scissors! The guy at Gone Fishing often came down to the dock with no tools; I felt like saying, "Get a cart and put a bag with bricks in it. At least then it looks like you have tools." If I ever professed to being a mechanic, I would always have an adjustable wrench and an electrical meter to check wires and voltage.)

Nonetheless, I was glad see this guy. He was a big, serious guy, like you'd imagine a baseball umpire would be. He was there to do a job. I liked that. He stated the obvious: that it was a classic boat that needed some heavy cleanup, especially if I was going to run charters (no shit!). I almost told him I'd been running charters for 10 years on complete shit boxes and that my phone would ring off the hook all summer long, thanks to Groupon.

Instead, I told him I wasn't worried about cosmetics as much as I was about the engine and transmission—how it shifted, how it sounded, how the engines were mounted, how the triggers looked, etc. When he heard the engines running, he said they looked okay; however, when we went out on the test run and the guy gave it some throttle, things started happening.

We left the hatch covers off the engines during the test drive. At first, I was amazed at how quickly the boat got up on a plane. The holeshot was amazing. I guess the torque of the diesels, combined with the turbos, really put the thing on a plane quick (maybe three seconds). I looked at my Navtronics on my phone, and we were going 19 knots, instantly—no laboring to get on a plane like outboards. I was so happy, maybe I had a winner after all. But then, oil started spitting and spewing out of one of the engine's blow-by hoses and steaming on the engine block, creating visible white smoke.

Obviously alarmed, the mechanic shrieked, "Stop!" But Joey, who was at the wheel, looked down, stopped the boat momentarily, saw the smoke, and shrugged it off. "That's from having too much oil" he calmly said. "It takes only three gallons. I put in three and a half by mistake. It will burn off; there is no issue."

Later, Joey explained that he had overfilled the engines before and they had done the same thing. Then, he drove slowly back to the dock. Another red flag—at this point, I must've lost track of how many there'd been. Overfilling an engine with oil should never happen once, let alone twice. A normal person would have walked away right there.

The mechanic left after being there a total of 15 minutes, saying to make sure Joey fixed the blow-by hose, since it could cause other major problems, like a leak in the pistons or a crack in the block, causing the oil to bypass a cylinder, which would eventually lead to catastrophic engine failure. It wasn't a good sign.

I was prepared to walk away from this cold bleak boatyard off the Belt Parkway with its dirty, abandoned project boats gone terribly wrong and its leaky Isuzu engines (speaking of which, when I ran model numbers of the engines in the boat, they came up as engines for "agricultural use"—in other words, tractor engines—and were awful for the Bertram deep-V hull design). If only I knew when to just walk away.

I told Joey that I was disappointed, that I wanted to buy it, and that I would come back if and when he fixed the problem.

But he was insistent. "Oh no, man, there is no problem! It was too much oil, I told you!" He went on and on about why it happened, how filling it with too much oil causes spills over the crankcase, and then out the hose, especially if the engines are at a weird tilt. The blow-by happened at 20 knots. All the oil that was going to burn off had already done so. He promised that if we took it out again, it would not smoke again. He guaranteed it. I wanted to believe him. So, we headed out again.

Once we cleared the marina's breakwater, Joey got her up on a plane. I watched the hose closely to see if any oil splattered out and, sure enough, there was no blow-by—no oil splattering out of the engine as before. The February rain was dense and cold. I went up to the bridge and watched the thermostats. They looked alright; we were not overheating. We headed in, and, once docked, I looked at the hose again. Joey was right, there was no oil coming out of the hole. Looking back, due to the rain, I don't think he pushed her the way he did first test drive.

I threw caution to the wind. I was sick of driving around and sick of looking. Someone always caves, either the buyer or the seller. I gave him $12k, citing that I was taking a huge risk with the blow-by problem and all. I told him if he had everything fixed in two weeks—the radar, the impellers, the oil changed, etc.—I would give him another $2k when I picked it up to drive it back to Montauk. We shook on it. I was sure that the extra $2k would be an incentive for the guy to fix it.

I was prepared to make the trip back to Montauk. I had made the run several times on various other boats by myself. But a friend convinced me that I shouldn't go alone on such an old boat at that time of year. She knew a great guy who fished all the time, just like me, albeit from the shore; she said he was "mechanically inclined," and if I offered him $100 bucks, he'd probably take the ride with me. She told me that he was a lot like me and we would get along, even saying that he may be the "yin to my yang."

I called the guy. We agreed on $200 plus bus fare back to NYC. He told me he had to be back by 10 p.m. for his friend's birthday party. I lied and told him he would probably make it.

After fighting heavy traffic on the Belt Parkway, and later on the side streets of Brooklyn, I arrived at the shithole that is Red Hook. Horribly marked streets, no GPS signal, a mess of warehouses and tenements. Stop signs. I had to pick him up because he didn't have a car and there was no public transportation to the boatyard. A cab would have been $40 bucks—in hindsight, I should've paid it. But the guy probably would not have been awake anyway. As it was, I woke him up at 10 a.m.

I was in a rush. There was weather coming to Montauk around 9 p.m. (20-knot east winds), so we needed leave by 12 p.m. to make it in six hours, ahead of the weather. At 16 knots, this would have been doable—the water was flat and calm—but we needed to get diesel fuel first. It had 30 gallons of fuel left in it, which had been sitting in the tank for at least two years.

I picked him up—he was a grungy little fellow. He had none of the tools I asked him to bring, and no hat or gloves. It was 35 degrees out, and we had a 120-mile ride on an open boat, driving from the bridge with only a 10-inch windshield. I had brought a face mask and goggles for myself, which we ended up sharing.

It turned out that this guy, probably in his mid-forties, lived in his mother's refurbished basement in Red Hook. As we drove to the yard, he filled me in on his story. He did not work; instead, he fished a lot and sold the PCB-laden striped bass he caught to people in the neighborhood. He'd been hit by a car while riding his bicycle 9 years before and had been waiting for a favorable settlement from the insurance company, which, he had just found out, had not panned out. He received exactly zero dollars from the case. Imagine—nine years in a holding pattern, living with his mom, to get nothing! Why was I always meeting people like this? . Before Groupon, most, if not all, of my customers had some kind of scam in the works: a workers' comp lawsuit about being trapped under a dumpster at work, or suing someone over getting rear ended at a stop sign. I'm not joking or exaggerating at all. I don't think I took anyone out fishing that was not collecting or waiting to collect on a settlement scam. None of them seemed legitimate.

I guess I attract these people. It's funny how losers seem to be drawn to other losers. It's like a magnet. Somehow, despite the millions of people in the world, we find each other! While I've had some nice pay days in my life , I've had to sponge off my family and sell fish without permits to get by. Very sad and pathetic, but true. My father has bought me five boats.

Back on the road with the grungy little fellow, I remember thinking as he was regaling me with his tale of woe., *Wow, I finally found one, this guy may well be a bigger loser than me.* Plus, he drank. He wanted me to buy six pack for the ride—not back to Montauk, to the boatyard!—to settle his nerves. It was 11 a.m. I said no. I needed him alert to help me check on the engines, and the temperature, and the fuel lines, and for the blow-by issue, and to ensure that the pumps were running. This was not going to be a joyride.

When we arrived at the yard, I saw the Bertram tied up at a floating dock. But Joey wasn't there. I tried calling and texting him—no response. Nothing. I had the title, I had insurance, I had already registered the boat and paid the $12k, but I had another $2k for him. Where the hell was he? We had scheduled this meetup. Didn't he want the extra $2k? Had he done the work to the boat that he said he was going to?

Joey was nowhere to be seen. The same Joey who told me before I bought the boat that he'd drive out to Montauk if it had any trouble—the same Joey who would service my boat with discount parts he got from the city. That guy who I wanted so desperately to trust was now MIA.

Me and the grungy guy walked down to the boat and kicked around it a bit. It was very cold. We wanted to start it, but we couldn't find a key. It didn't look like Joey had changed the fuel filters, which was critical because they could easily clog with old fuel. Finally, a young guy came down to the boat and told us that Joey could not be there do to work, but if we had any questions, he could help.

I asked where the key was. As it turned out, the boat had no key! There was a button you pushed after holding down the booster to warm and loosen the old diesel fuel. We made sure that the water pump was pushing water out of both hoses off the stern (they were), and we pushed off the dock for our voyage east. We managed to find a fueling station down what looked like an abandoned creek. I remember being in two feet of water at times down this canal. I also remember the eerie, sad reminders of Hurricane Sandy: piles of debris, abandoned buildings, gutted buildings still not finished, despite 10 years having passed.

There was a break in the weather, so we had to move fast. The wind was supposed to blow nonstop for the rest of week. We got 100 gallons of fuel, then we went under Verrazano-Narrows Bridge, banged a left out of the jetties, and headed east toward Montauk.

At first, to my surprise and delight, the boat rode great right up on a plane. We were doing 18 knots. The guy took the first shift; he wore my hat and ski goggles. I sat in the cabin and took videos on my phone of the wake. The sun was out, and the water was flat and calm. Coney Island Beach and the famous Ferris wheel and Parachute Jump passed by our port side. I posted something stupid on Facebook, like: "19 knots no problem, Canyon here we come!" I was happy. And it looked like I had saved $2k! The engines sounded great—maybe this boat really was a steal after all. I gloated to friends on the phone. None of them thought I would make it the 120 miles; many had even bet against it. I didn't care that my phone battery was down to 20 percent and the charger on board was not working. I was so happy. Finally, after being ripped off by more deals on Craiglist than I cared to remember, I had found a good one: a Bertram 28 with diesels for $12k.

Things went well for around 25 miles, up until we got to, I guess, Jones Inlet. When the port engine began to bog down, the guy took the engine hatch off and looked at the filter. It looked clogged, and there was water building up in the hull. Were the bilge pumps even working? If so, they weren't working well. Nothing was coming out of the side. On top of this, the starboard engine was blowing some very familiar white smoke.

More water was in the bilge than there'd been when we left. It did not look like much to me, maybe two inches, but I now know that two inches displaced could be 100 gallons.

The guy wanted to abort the trip immediately. He was afraid the boat was taking on water and unsafe, and he demanded that we take it in to Jones Inlet and have someone look at it. What this guy didn't know was that unless this monstrosity completely stalled and sank, I was determined to push it to Montauk. Why? Because so many people were betting that I wouldn't make it to Montauk in this shit bomb, and because so many people told me not to buy it in the first place and that it would never make it back to Montauk. I had to prove them wrong.

I told my scared comrade that I was not familiar with Jones Inlet, but if we pushed it another 20 miles to Fire Island Inlet, I would take it in there. The port engine stalled out a bit, but then kicked back in. It surged and lurched. We were down to around 10 knots, but we were moving. About an hour away from the Fire Island Inlet, a sea tow boat and Coast Guard cutter passed us; I was reassured.

I tried to pump up my depressed and now reluctant crew member.

"Look," I pointed enthusiastically stating, "There are Coast Guard boats and sea tow boats all around us. Both of our phones work. The VHF radio works. If we break down, I'll call both of them."

Because it was starting to get foggy, he was not reassured. Panic and anger were in his eyes.

"Let's push it to Moriches Inlet," I said, "I know some mechanics there." Though true, I let Moriches come and go, hoping the guy wouldn't notice. He did. And when he saw that I wasn't turning into the inlet, he protested. I told the guy that Moriches has too many sand bars (in fact, it's marked as navigable waters on all the charts) and that we'd surely run aground. Best to press on to the Shinnecock Inlet, the next one. The guy was inconsolable.

"Dude, this boat is not safe," he bellowed. "It's 45-degree water; if this other engine craps out, we're going to sink!"

We limped along for another hour, not speaking. When we got to the Shinnecock Inlet, I refused to go in, saying we only had another 38 miles to Montauk Point. We were down to just the port engine, running at 6 knots. It was 7 p.m. and dark. If we broke down, we'd be crushed by the impending storm. The guy opened the engine hatch; the water had gone up to three inches, now rising to the engine block.

"Pull it in right now! Beach it! This thing's not seaworthy. We're taking water on and only have one engine. The water is freezing; if this thing sinks, we will drown."

Looking back, he was right on all counts. My cell had died... his had 30 percent. But my ego made us push on.

"We can make it at 7 knots," I told him. "We can make it in two hours ahead front."

"What are you insane?" he said. "We are going to drown!"

Finally, I looked at him and calmly, directly said, "Look, look at us. Look at the predicament we're in. You're living on your mother's couch, and I'm stuck with this shit box of a boat, pretending I'm a charter boat captain." And then I added, and really, truly meant it, "Would it be the worst thing for civilization if two striped bass poaching losers went down at sea?"

"You're fucking crazy" he yelled.

He went to sulk in the cabin. I pushed on as I said I would, covering the 38 miles at 7 knots on one sputtering engine (the other had stalled long ago). We limped into Montauk around 10 p.m. The wind was just picking up. At the dock, we did a half-ass job of tying up my new craft (the owner of the dock wondered who would leave their boat like that, then he remembered I was coming to town), and I raced him to the train station. We barely missed the last train to NYC, so I let him stay at my condo at

Montauk Manor while I stayed on my boat. We never spoke again.

The mechanic at the marina looked at the engine right away. I'd once been great friends with everyone at this marina. But this boat, coupled with my wild ego, would test and eventually ruin every relationship I had built there. My boat was leaking oil, so the owners of the marina wanted it out of there. I tried to sell it for $3,000, but no one would drive to Montauk, even just to look at it.

It was impossible to find a mechanic in Montauk that would work on a diesel engine, especially an Isuzu. I called and called and called. One guy said he'd come once the traffic died down in Southampton, which was like saying once hell freezes over. I could not give the thing away.

So, I started to take charters out on one engine.

As it turned out, the owners of the marina were selling their shares that very year; the deal was going down, sale pending. The last thing they needed was me or my shitty boat around to blow the deal. I can't blame them. They could've gotten major fines for oil in the water. However, the owner kept this from me. If he had spelled it out like that, I would not have had a problem.

After a huge fight, I pulled out of Gone Fishing Marina for good and went to Diamond Cove Marina, otherwise known as "the place dreams go to die."

There, I ran charters on one engine for most of the summer.

Chapter 9

Other Googan Captains

My friend "Captain" Pat had the nerve to claim on his Groupon profile that he was a shark fisherman, even though he'd only done it maybe five times on other people's boats. Customers contacted him, dates were set, and he took deposits on his Apple Pay. They'd take Pat's 33-foot seaworthy Grady-White (in good repair) to the shark grounds, 20 miles south off Montauk Point. Unlike the filthy, unsafe scam of an operation I ran, he had all the right safety equipment.

On one particular trip, the weather report was fair but not ideal, calling for light winds but from the east. East winds are never good in Montauk for many reason ("east is least, west is best," as the saying goes). It was supposed pick up to 15 to 20 knots later that night, but they would be back at the dock by that point, he hoped.

Fifteen to 20 knot winds from the east are rough, but they're certainly not a hurricane. I've been caught in 30-knot winds probably over 20 times in 21 to 25-foot boats and made it home. It wasn't pleasant: I took a beating, got wet, but it wasn't a nail biter, like trying to find an airport runway on a foggy day with no navigational instruments.

Unfortunately for Pat, the weather that had been predicted to come later that night arrived sooner than expected. And Pat, witnessing the waves growing to four to five feet (large but manageable), instantly went into panic mode. In direct earshot of his customers, he said stuff to the mate like, "This is bad, this real bad," and "I've never seen it this bad." Of course, the captain shouldn't show fear in any circumstances, right? Even if he has to fake confidence. When I find myself in rough weather, I try to make fun of it, even if I'm scared shitless and disappointed that I've put my customers in harm's way. I hide it and say, "Weeeee!" and "Thank you, sir, may I have another?" as we drop five foot waves and take the next one over the bow, getting soaked in the process.

Instead, Pat told his mate to reel in the rods and that they were cutting the trip short and heading home. He commanded the customers to put on life preservers, which was okay, but the terror in his voice was alarming. They rode home at 10 knots and were doing fine. Sure, there was wind, and they were rolling around some, and some five to six foot waves were coming over the bow. Unpleasant for sure, but manageable.

In Montauk, northeast winds can turn the sea into a washing machine. The waves become unpredictable and roll in from different directions, so it's tough to find any pattern to them. Pat had certainly never seen this scenario before, and the fact that he was 20 miles offshore put him into a full-on panic. He alerted the Coast Guard that he was coming into heavy seas and gave them his coordinates, which caused the (until now) calm customers to show some visible distress. And then Pat uttered these words: "Hold on tight, and be on the lookout for rogue waves." Rogue waves? That's like a pilot in bad weather getting on the intercom and asking the passengers to be on the lookout for mountain tops, trees, and radio towers. It's just not a great plan unless you're trying to breed hysteria.

It got worse.

Finally, now completely panic stricken, Pat found it necessary to deploy his six-man emergency rescue raft. The mate tried to talk him out of it, but Pat insisted. It took the mate a while to figure out which rope to pull to instantly inflate the eight-foot life raft, and when the thing finally opened, it happened so abruptly that it almost pushed one the customers off the side of the boat. The life raft now occupied most of the cockpit area, leaving nowhere for the now horrified customers to sit. It was sheer pandemonium.

They made it to the harbor in three hours. It was free trip, of course, though the mate got a tip. Worst of all, it cost Pat over $1,000 to get his life raft repacked (he had to send it out somewhere). Now, 10 years later, Pat is a fine captain, and he's not afraid of a northeast blow. By the way, I've put customers through far, far worse than this, by comparison, relatively minor episode. At least Pat's customers didn't sue. My point is, I was not the only googan captain out there.

There are plenty of stories about boats getting close to shore and capsizing. One friend of mine got a rope caught in the prop of his 26-foot Fortier and told his customers to jump in the water before a wave flipped them. The boat, pushed by the incoming tide, crashed right into the lighthouse and got lodged on the rocks. At low tide, it was high and dry for all to see. It took three days to salvage the boat, which basically became a tourist attraction until then.

Years ago, another one of my "captain" friends had someone like the chairman of the National Fly Fishing Association or Fly Fisher International or whatever onboard as a single passenger on a small 20-foot May-Craft skiff. As boiling bass corralled the disoriented bait in the whitewash behind the crashing waves, my friend would keep the boat headed into the waves and run up them when they were about to breach. Sure, it was risky, but he'd done it a million times. On this particular day, "the chairman" had a fish on his line, and when my friend went back to unhook the fish, he looked up just in time to a see a big wave crashing over them. It was too late. There was nothing he could do. The little boat flipped. The boat was totaled, as was the poor captain's career. The fishing world may be small, but the fly fishing world is even smaller. There are certain things you can't do—like flip your boat with a high profile customer onboard—if you want to maintain a thriving charter boat business.

*

I have always admitted that I don't deserve a boat—a beating, perhaps, but not a boat.

My father bought me my first boat and had me make the $210 monthly payments. I may have made the first two, and then he had to take over. Of course, life is unfair, so I kept the boat anyway.

I am a WASP. Generally, WASPs wait to inherit their money and various neurological diseases (hopefully in that order). There are exceptions. My mother and sisters, for instance, are both hardworking. But most WASPs, it would seem, are in a perpetual holding pattern, just circling and circling, waiting for someone die, and then fighting over the money.

As for me, I *should* be drifting around in a pool on a tube in a structured living environment, not running a charter boat in Montauk (move over, Dad. Who's the one in a nursing home now?). I live in a condo my mother bought for me in Montauk Manor—an old historic hotel perched on top of a hill, dramatically overlooking the sea at the end of the southern tip of Long Island. With its small functional units and elevators, Montauk Manor would make a great structured living environment or retirement home. The only problem is it's not close enough to a hospital (30 miles away in Southampton) and too far for family members to visit (actually, that may be a selling point).

Montauk was once hailed the "Sportfishing Capital of the World." It is home to a gorgeous and infamous fleet of charter boats; neither I nor my boat belong to this auspicious fraternity. Nevertheless, with the help of Groupon, for a couple of years anyway, I was busier than them all.

***

It can't be overstated enough: There are many "captains" out there who have no real sea time or experience. They simply wanted the charter boat "captain" title, so they took a crash course (now available online for $700), memorized a bunch of answers (many of which are now obsolete), and passed a test for their valid USCG captain's credential. Consequently, they are now licensed and insured to take people out for hire. It's my belief that many of these "captains," myself included, should not be allowed to take people out for money until they pass an additional practical hands-on portion of the exam that demonstrates their nautical prowess at sea. Yes, you can memorize the road rules, but can you back a single crew boat into a slip or anchor a vessel?

I remember getting fired from a Wall Street job many years ago. Although he probably thought I was a rock head, my supervisor liked me. And I believe he meant well when told me something to the tune of, "Look, you're not cut out for this type of white-collar work. You love fishing and you're good at it. It's your passion, so why don't you get a little boat out in Montauk and take tourists fishing? And in the winter, do it in Florida." In fact, a few people had told me this. It sounded nice and simple enough, but even then, I knew it couldn't be that easy. Though well intended, these people were grossly uninformed about what it took to be a successful captain.

I suppose I've always respected blue-collar over white-collar work. There was a book (I forget the title—maybe *Bonfire of the Vanities*?) where the protagonist—a bond trader in a nice corner office in a New York City high-rise—gets in trouble. Anyway, his entire world is imploding and he's feeling the pressure as he looks down at the East River and observes a tugboat making its way north, pulling some freight. He says (or thinks) something along the lines of, "Ah, I wish I was that guy in the tugboat, a simple life, not a care in the world, just a guy and a boat trying to get from point A to point B up the river."

I remember reading this and being taken back. What was he thinking? That tugboat captain is under far more stress than the financial guy. The captain is probably hoping that his fuel filter doesn't clog, causing his big Detroit diesel engine to stall, allowing his barge full of cement cargo that he was transporting up to New Paltz to get pulled back by the strong 10-knot East River current and careening into one of the support pillars off the 59th Street Bridge. Sure, the guy in the office might do some soft white-collar prison time, but the tugboat captain could conceivably level the 59th Street Bridge. So who's got more pressure?

The point is, the guy in the office has no concept of the waterman's pressures and responsibilities. Commercial fishing, which includes charter boat fishing, is one of the hardest professions on earth.

***

Back to *Do What You Love, The Money Will Follow.* Think of all the ridiculous, dead-end pilgrimages to nowhere that book put people on, not to mention all the restaurants, galleries, and surf shops that were opened and closed soon after—all the dashed dreams. Sad when the poor enthusiast realizes that loving a hobby does not often translate into making it a profitable business. There, of course, are wonderful exceptions. I don't want to discourage someone from following his dream. However, future wannabe captains, please listen . . . if you want to get into the charter fishing game, go to mechanical school first.

Yes, I loved to fish, and because I did it all the time, I got good at it. What makes a good fisherman, you ask? Time! That is, no commitments. If you're a heavy partier, you will probably lose at this sport. Knowing the tides and winds is also critical, as is tying the right rigs, figuring out what foriging on called, "matching the hatch," and about a hundred other things, including developing the right instincts. For example, how quick can you retie a line to line line? How often should you check your line? How well can you fight the fish while precisely anchoring on wrecks (if you're two feet off, you might not catch at all)? It's all about doing it, over and over and over again. If you're out drinking and chasing girls, you probably won't last long in Montauk—maybe three or four years, then you will burn out or get tossed out. In almost 20 years, I have seen many aspiring charter fishermen come and go.

It's not about money; money can't make a fish bite your hook. While fishing, I've had fishermen anchor 300 feet from me in their six-figure Yellowfin boats run by professional captains and geared up with the best rods you can buy. After watching me bail fish after fish for an hour, they had to pull anchor and leave. Money can't buy fishing ability, only time can. However, in the end, though we would like you to believe otherwise, there are no rock stars in the fishing business. It doesn't matter how good you are or you think you are; if the fish are not there, if the ecosystem is not strong; if there are not regulations in force, then make no mistake, no one will catch them. The fish are the only true rock stars of this sport, and that's why conservation is paramount. Let's try not to forget this.

Chapter 10

Sloth

I'm a nice enough guy, but I've got to admit, I'm a slob! My condition far transcends messy and disorganized. I am a chronic slob, or what they affectionately called in rural parts of Texas, a "clusterfuck." My sloppiness does not make sense; it's nasty and vile. It surpasses average lazy sloppiness like leaving clothes on the floor or dirty dishes in the sink (although I do both). My sloth manifests in bizarre behavior like dashing out a cigarette in a girlfriend's new $100 bottle of moisturizer (tough to explain, right?) or hoarding a six-week-old pizza box with a few slices, a W-2 form, and a random sock like it's a work of art. Yeah, that kind slob.

Oftentimes, sloppy people are more affable and funny, funnier than neat people for sure. I think of John Belushi in *Animal House*. I used to joke about my hygiene in my comedy act—"If I had a Virginia it would stink." Sloppiness is funny but not an asset when trying to run a boat and attract customers. On the other side of the spectrum, compulsively neat people are kind of scary, too. You know that person who's constantly cleaning, even when you come to visit:

"So, Jane, what are you doing over your vacation?"

"Well, just cleaning a lot and organizing my underwear draw."

Don't let clean freaks fool you—it's not a burden to them, and it's not their incredible work ethic. They find comfort and safety in cleaning. By doing it, they feel protected from life's inevitable cruelties. They'd rather clean and do laundry than interact with people.

In the end, when all is said and done, it's better to be neat and clean than a slob. Especially when running a boat, and especially when you take people out on it for money. Being a slob is funny, no doubt, but not *that* funny.

While I am, indeed, lazy by nature, in my defense, my childhood was not conducive to blue-collar mechanical work. I grew up on Manhattan's Upper East Side in the early 1970s. My mom was an artist, and my dad a writer for the *New York Times*.

My father's meager aptitude with basic carpentry was not passed on to me. Relying on the subway system, we had no cars, so we had no need or interest to work on them. At 15 years old, I had no idea what a socket wrench was. Very few (if any) Manhattan kids have to trailer off-road utility vehicles. We didn't have boats and RVs, we had no trailer to maintain; we didn't even have a lawn to cut. Our building had superintendents who did all the work. Come to think of it, I'm not sure what we did with our free time. I know we had skateboards and played ping-pong. I played the game, *Tron*, at the local corner store, and I had gay sex a few times, but that's off topic.

Quite frankly, unless you were a music or sports prodigy, most of us NY kids just hung around. I do remember getting mugged a lot; NYC was a brutal place in the late 1970s under Mayor Ed Koch. People got mugged all the time—and I mean all the fucking time. It was common to see some guy grab a lady's purse and take off down the street. We emptied our pockets many times for packs of urban youths. Ask how many graduates of Trinity School—an Ivy League Prep School in Manhattan's the Upper West Side—can hitch a trailer and tow a 30-foot boat a hundred miles or do the essential maintenance such as lubricating bearings, changing hubs, and the answeris probably zero!

At my liberal arts college, Hobart, perched on the northwest corner of Seneca Lake in Geneva, New York there was no focus on basic mechanics. There were plenty of useless anthropology classes that we all signed up for; I may still be able to give a somewhat adequate description of what a nomadic tribe is. But I was not taught how to change fuses, test and clean a battery, clean terminals, test a new alternator or starter. This stuff is essential not just in boating but in all of life. College has everyone rushing into law or finance (particularly hedge funds) law and public relations, and if you didn't get into one of these fields, you were fucked. Looking back, I wish I'd joined the Coast Guard or become a cop, but upper middle-class kids just didn't do that. For good or for bad, we were white-collar bound.

I'm sick of calling men to fix stuff at my house. YouTube videos help with some stuff, of course, but I'm basically fucked. When the engine on my boat stalls, I go through the mute and largely ceremonial exercise of taking off the cover, staring at it a bit, and resisting the temptation of throwing poo at it like an orangutan at the zoo. Then, I call Sea Tow.

The charter boat fleet in Montauk is one of the best in the world. Truth be told, I had some nerve trying to join them. My chronic sloppiness and lack of mechanical skills have rendered me ill-equipped as a charter boat captain—a business where the margin of profit compared to overhead is huge. Captains have to be resourceful and find ways to save and not spend money. A lot of this involves preventative maintenance and making our own rigs. All the vessels in Montauk are well maintained and gorgeous; if you're ever out there, drive by the harbor and look at some (or look them up on the Internet: the *Hooker*, *Adah-K*, *Adios*, *Herl's Girl*, *Blue Fin IV*, *Vivienne*, *Sea Wife IV*, *Lady Grace V*, *Susie E II*, *Grand Slam*). I can see why these charter captains did not want a Mosquito Fleet of weekend warrior hacks taking their business away simply because they took a crash course at sea school for $700.

Those courses suck. You know what they should do at sea school? They should just show videos of horrible boating accidents, one after another. Candidates would get scared, drop out, and return to their day jobs as dentists or accountants.

*

My enthusiasm for fishing took me a long way. Twice, on my own small charter boat, customers caught the largest striped bass in Montauk, weighing 54 and 55 pounds. Twice, I received $500 tips from elated customers who had been trying to catch an elusive 50 pounder for many years. I have taken celebrities out . . . okay, just one: Chad Smith, the drummer for the Red Hot Chili Peppers. I caught the largest bass and shark at the Gone Fishing Marina for seven out of my 15 years there.

Long before Groupon, I advertised discount trips on Craigslist (no shortage of losers on that site). I illegally sold fish to restaurants and would also get huge food and drink credits; I rarely used these credits, however, because I was always on the water and my hygiene was so bad I couldn't even imagine entering a nice restaurant or even an outdoor bar. The few times I did use a credit, I'd bring in big groups of people, mostly younger Bulgarians who worked for the Viking Fleet. The bill would come to over $1,000, and we'd simply leave $100 tip for the waiter.

I was having a lot of fun, and I was so happy. The only people I imagined could be happier than me were rock stars— yes, a rock star might've been having more fun than me, but, then again, they were probably practicing music cooped in the studio and not outside fishing, like me.

Like I said earlier, when I first got to Montauk, I'd hear captains on the VHF radio, and they all sounded miserable. I remember thinking, "Why do they all sound so bleak? They get to fish every day!" Now, 10 years later, I get it—boy, do I get it!

To really make a living in the fishing business—not a weekend warrior like I was—is a day-to-day grind. It takes a lot patience, hard work, and extreme resourcefulness. For instance, salt is extremely corrosive, so constant preventative maintenance is paramount.

Every boat I ever owned, however, was a disaster and a health risk. I use to joke with my customers that they had a good chance of catching huge fish and hepatitis C at the same time! My anchor line was often too short and tangled with a mess of fishing line. Debris would often clog my only working bilge pump. Though they stunk of bleach that I liberally poured all over them, my boats were never clean. I was pulled in and saved by the Coast Guard at least seven times (they always did a great job; I owe them more than one of my lives). My running lights worked sporadically, and my VHF radios were always on the fritz. The endless fines and citations I'd receive for all of this cut into any profit I might have made as a captain. It was big joke for me. It was funny—fucking hysterical—but, in the end, I guess the joke was on me, and things really start to lose their humor when someone ends up getting hurt.

***

According to Murphy's Law, whatever can go wrong will go wrong. And Murphy was definitely at the helm the time I invited a popular manager from the prestigious East Hampton Gym to fish with me on my boat for free. I had been regaling him with stories and pictures of huge fish all summer, and I was hoping that he would witness and partake in some great fishing and tell everyone who walked into his busy gym what a great time he'd had on my boat and what a tremendous fisherman I was and they should book with me immediately (that is, if I still had any openings).

So, one night, after my customers and I had caught close to 30 big bass—some over 40 pounds—I called the gym manager and told him to come the next night. The tide would be the same, incoming: "The bite was on, and the fish were there." My plan was foolproof.

The following night, when the gym manager came, I had a Groupon charter booked with some Spanish guys, and I had just declared that my friend was coming along. There were only three of them, and they had no problem with one more person tagging along. We left at 5 p.m., and the fish were biting on the incoming tide just at dusk. The striped bass were chewing as anticipated; this was going to be easy. Every boat around us was hooked up already, and people were literally cheering!

We started getting hits right away, but when the customers went to set the hook, the line snapped, and we lost the entire rig: sinker, swivel, leader, and hook. Confused by this, I retied the line and had the gym manager drive the boat back up to where the fish were. It took five minutes to get each rod ready. I got them all set up with new rigs, and we ran back up on the drift and dropped down. BAM! We got hit again. But then, just like the first time, the line snapped again. Finally, I realized that the ceramic inserts lining the guide eyes on my rods had broken off, so exposed metal was fraying and eventually cutting the monofilament line. My fault entirely.

We were losing the tide, so I had to work quickly. I changed all the rods and reels out to old backups and put brand new line on them, which took about 30 minutes. I tried to remain calm, but we were wasting critical fishing time, and I didn't want my customers—and, particularly, the gym manager—to miss out on this amazing opportunity. We could still get a few more passes at the fish before they stopped biting. Big bass don't generally feed in slack water, and the bite can stop abruptly. It's like a dinner bell: fish feed at precise times, and then stop just as quickly.

We ran back up on the drift. All we could hear and see were customers on other boats hooting and hollering and having a great time landing monster bass. Finally, the gym manager hooked into a nice one, and, for a brief moment, we all got excited as the fish was peeling off line. Seconds later, things took a bad turn. Maybe the drag was too loose, but the guy couldn't keep the fish off the bottom, and the big female bass got him into the boulder fields. The 50-pound fluorocarbon leader, in its usual manner, exploded on the first rock it touched (that shit has no abrasion resistance at all, despite what it says on the label. It does not get nicked off or fray—it just explodes). So, the gym manager lost his trophy fish and went home with no pictures to show. My PR campaign was a bust.

Fortunately, no real damage had been done. That was the fifth fish we lost, and now I was yelling and cursing! If just one of the Spanish guys hooked up, it could have saved the whole trip. But no, the old backup reel had some kind of bird's nest or bad drag, and the line broke off that one, too. After we'd lost seven fish, I forced myself to calm down, retied a third time, and ran back up. By that time, unfortunately, the tide was shot; only 20 minutes before, all the boats that had been celebrating their huge catches went quiet. The bight was over. People on other boats were taking pictures of their catches, high fiving, and going home. I was so angry that I took all four rods, smashed them one by one, and tossed them over the side of the boat in front of the bewildered customers and, worse, the manager of the East Hampton Gym!

So now, not only did the manager of the gym *not* send me any customers, he also told everyone I was a fucking lunatic.

Oftentimes, and especially in offshore fishing, when the stakes are high, there's is a cunt hair-size line between catching and not catching. The results are all in the details and prep work.

Chapter 11

Shot Out of a Cannon

I guess it's no surprise that I tried to become a Montauk charter boat captain (possibly one the most elite and respected fleets in the history of the sportfishing industry). I have had a history of pursuing irresponsible, grandiose careers for which I was remarkably unsuited and under-qualified. Standup comedy, for one. I was clever enough, even pithy, but my speech was slurred and garbled, bordering on inarticulate, and I was very nervous on stage. Despite all this, I still managed to incorporate myself into the industry to some degree, working here and there and opening for some big celebrities. Just like with fishing, I had my moments.

I suppose I was always in search of fame and recognition; we all are, to an extent, but I took it to an extreme. I bet back in the 1900s, when it was a good and legitimate job (as outdoor circus and county fairs drew thousands), I would have been well suited for being shot out of a cannon, although I don't know the exact criteria for pursuing a career as a human cannonball. It's hard to imagine that being shot out of a cannon would require a whole lot of talent; all you'd really have to do is get in the cannon and, once shot, remember to wave at the cheering crowd who are probably secretly hoping that the cannon would misfire, overshoot the landing net, and send your imbecilic corpse careening over the parking lot and splattering in an unrecognizable mess into the waffle truck. This would invoke more cheers and possibly a standing ovation, for sure!

***

Somehow, I graduated from Hobart College on the northeast corner of Seneca Lake in the Finger Lakes region of New York (I'm still not sure how this happened; all I did was cheat, do drugs, and drink). At the time in the mid-eighties, Hobart was one of the top five men's lacrosse schools in the country. Saying you played varsity lacrosse at Hobart in the '80s would be like claiming you made it to the semifinals of the French Open. In other, words it was a distinguished and elite field.

Although I had some athletic prowess in high school, I also attended a small special education boarding school for affluent families who wanted (or needed) to warehouse their wayward children. Had she not been callously lobotomized, Rosemary Kennedy would have made a good candidate for the Forman School since they didn't medicate their students (although I can see why they do now—Adderall can turn a C student into an A student almost overnight). Forman's varsity teams would play other schools' JV and thirds teams. To say that I was a big fish in a small pond was an understatement. Out of only 200 students (some of whom, god bless them, used walkers), making the cut was a snap.

But at Hobart, I was nowhere near qualified to play for their lacrosse team. As a Division III school, my alma mater competed with Duke, John Hopkins, and Syracuse. It wasn't until I was 41 years old that I told anyone I played lacrosse at Hobart (often rounding out the edges of this blatant lie by saying I'd played on the B team). In my defense, and in the name of candor, I did play in a couple of club games that were no joke since they had some fifth-year seniors that used to play varsity. I will say I had very strong legs for never working out; I probably would've been a good enough running back. I laid one guy out hard in one of those club games, all thanks to the fact that, in boarding school, all you do is wrestle.

And speaking of wrestling: One Groupon trip, I had two 45-year-old guys who played college football at Syracuse in the '80s and went on to play preseason for the Giants. On top of this, their kids were starting to play Division I ball—one at Boston College, the other at Rutgers. Another guy was the coach of Rhode Island football. Point is, they were jocks. Their life was sports, and they had played at the highest organized levels.

I was impressed by them, but I also felt a little emasculated. I was basically cut from the JV soccer team in high school. So, they were talking football, and somehow, I was overcome by the need to announce that I had been a "GREAT wrestler in school."

Yes . . . I said that. I kind of just blurted it out.

Before it even left my mouth, I knew it was a mistake. I hadn't played football, but I was pretty strong for a little guy— five foot ten, 175 pounds—and I still believe I was a great wrestler in school, which is subject to interpretation. When I was in boarding school, kids would start to spontaneously wrestle during free time or passing in the hallway. Usually, it was good spirited, but it could get intense, with real "tap outs." I must say, I'd had a few moves, and I was pretty good at getting people to the ground. I loved wrestling! Later, in college, I would get drunk and antagonize football players. I could pin a lot of them, even the ones who were obviously on steroids. The guys who could usually throw me around were hockey players, so I learned to stay away from them. I certainly was not, by any standard, a great college or high school wrestler. I'd never been on an organized team. So, when I called myself a "GREAT wrestler," I guess I meant that I had a great enthusiasm and aptitude for spontaneous roughhousing.

Anyway, my football-pro customers were impressed. They knew I was a good fisherman and assumed that, by "GREAT wrestler," I was talking about real accolades I had earned in high school or NCAA competitive wrestling, and maybe even the Olympic trials. The customers perked up and started to pepper me with questions. Did I make it to the regionals? What weight class? College or high school? Did I tour? I had to stop them with one the most awkward explanations ever: "Oh no, no, guys, sorry I was not clear. I did not wrestle on an organized team. I didn't do it competitively. I would just wrestle with friends, you know? Just for fun, like in the hallway." As if that wasn't enough, I proceeded to act out my "GREAT" wrestling by pretending to get someone in a headlock. "You know? Get the guy in a headlock, and he tries to squirm out, and he can't, and finally he yells uncle?" They looked disgusted, confused, and embarrassed. I may as well have told them hooking fish gave me a hard on.

***

Back to lacrosse: One day, in a moment of clarity, I abruptly stopped telling people that I played lacrosse in college. What a relief; it was getting me nowhere. Why was I saying it? It never got me laid or earned me a job. I remember watching people's faces as they struggled to grapple with trying to visualize what, indeed, a lacrosse player was—like, maybe someone chugging cheap keg beer while his friend raped a prostitute? Some wondered if it was a good thing or a bad thing. One of my first jokes I wrote as a comedian was about lacrosse:

"A lot of kids have sex in college. That's the time to do it, although parents pay thirty grand a year so their kids can drink and try to fuck. Not in my case: Seven years of college, I only got one hand job. Granted he was on the lacrosse team, but still . . ."

Another friend, knowing that, despite being good natured and funny, I was extremely learning disabled, had a poor work ethic, and was also a complete burnout after toasting my brain with designer drugs and acid in college. Just about every weekend, I tripped on something. I was struggling to find a job in New York, in part because of my love for pickup basketball. I played every day at the local YMCA and was not shy about joining any game (despite frequent complaints from disgruntled team mates). Back to lacrosse. I had modest ability but lacked a basic grasp of the game other than run and shoot. I must say that occasionally my weak and anemic shots went down and we did win a few games.

When I was out of college and looking for a job I asked a friend if he thought I could coach: he thought about it for a second and then, fondly and playfully suggested that I would make a great woman's JV intramural volleyball coach.

That, I suppose, helped lead me into another one of my first standup comedy jokes:

"When I got out of college, I took one of those career aptitude tests. You know, the ones that assess your skills and tell you what field you should pursue, like doctor, lawyer, or accountant? Well, I took the test and the results indicated that I would make an outstanding hunter-gatherer."

While most of the jobs I shot for were high profile (the Goldman Sachs and Merrill Lynch training programs, for example—my mom had contacts and pushed hard, not afraid to drop my grandfather's name; both were captains of industry), not all were grandiose. Some were just silly and unrealistic.

For instance, I decided I wanted to fundraise for nonprofit organizations. How tough could that be? After taking an eight-week grant writing course at The New School in Manhattan, I prepared my resume. In the years prior to this, I had worked as a telemarketer for Covenant House—a nonprofit that offers shelter and direction to runaway teens. They gave us carrels with a phone and lists of numbers. None of the donors wanted to hear from us; it was a miserable job. I made a lot of personal calls, laughed with the director, and napped. Anyway, I put this on my resume and fudged some more stuff, I'm sure. I had no idea of the detailed work involved in fundraising, bookkeeping, scheduling events, creating spreadsheets, making prospective goals, etc. With one course under my belt and only the vaguest notion of all the tasks a fundraiser requires—did they throw parties?—I applied for the director of fundraising position at nonprofit cancer research organization in Queens, if I recall correctly. It also could have been the Boys & Girls Club of America. Whatever it was, I was under-qualified for the job.

The day of the interview, I put on my power broker Hugo Boss shirt (my sister used to work there) and designer suit. I have to admit, I looked great. Right before I was called into the interview, I went in front of the mirror and threw some fake pitches to get my blood flowing and look athletic—get a little pumped up going alpha male. I was an optimist, a go getter! The director of fundraising had a nice ring to it and might lead me into bigger things like politics.

I was about five minutes into the interview, giving my spiel, when the interviewer, a serious professional woman, stopped me and, in a matter of fact tone, asked, "Excuse me, but why did you apply for this job?"

I told her the truth: I liked the idea of raising money for worthy causes.

"That was all well and good," she explained, "but this position, director of fundraising, is very specific, and you need to be well versed on all aspects of fundraising from grant writing to phone banks, alumni giving, annual reports, federal grant writing, tax issues, etc."

In other words, I would need years of experience to be considered for the job. I suppose I misread the ad to mean "fun-raising."

She concluded that I was, in her words, "Unrealistically optimistic and remarkably under-qualified for the position." This stuck with me.

Chapter 12

Jimmy George and His Spoon

In 2004, I had a little piece of shit 22-foot Angler with a two-stroke Suzuki 225 outboard. But somehow, I eked out a modest living—$15,000 per year after expenses. On the side, I took jobs mating with popular and notorious captains. I learned the business and how to cut fish. I worked on the Viking fluke-fishing boat for six solid weeks (I was not fired, party boats never fire people, you show up and they don't take you). I did some commercial fishing on a dragger (I loved it—the industry and hard work; my first week doing it, I thought I'd found my career, but I hated the bycatch waste). I also did some hook and line ("pin hooking") fishing for bass and fluke on various commercial boats, often working 18-hour days.

In 2008 and 2009, way before I even considered using Groupon, I had some success in Montauk working as a mate on a very busy and notorious charter boat, the *Nicole Marie*, with Captain Jimmy George. Jimmy had invented something called a "Secret Spoon," which resembled a giant (up to 2.5 pounds) bunker spoon; it looked more like a fluke or flounder than anything else. It was a smart design because, at the time, due to the high demand of omega-3 fish oil, companies were eradicating the menhaden (bunker) population with pair seine draggers and, as a result, wiping out the main food source for striped bass. There had been an abundance of striped bass in 2003, but, without much bait around other than peanut bunker and sand eels, the big bass fed on anything they could find, like lobster, fluke, and flounder. In 2004 the fish reached Montauk and were starving, they would eat anything. Jimmy's spoon came around at a good time for the customer, and a bad time for the fish.

Jimmy worked like crazy on these spoons. In his basement in New Jersey, which resembled a Detroit manufacturing plant, he had a kiln, ovens, special airbrush paints, and stacks of sheet metal that he relentlessly pounded for hours at a time. When orders for his spoon increased and he needed another oven, he cut a hole in his kitchen wall and used that oven, and he installed a shoot that slid the hot metal down into his basement. It was all very elaborate; I'm glad I got to see it once in operation. When he first brought the spoon to Montauk in June 2003, every big striped bass in the Northeast showed up at Montauk Point for the summer. And, in those years, there was not a lot of bait around.

While cleaning striped bass that summer, I remember finding large skate fish and lobsters in their stomachs. They would eat anything. Including, apparently, the entire flounder population. On top of that, working with the spoon was dangerous business. Often, it would get loose and swing around like a medieval weapon. Jimmy also had me retrieve the metal slab in all kinds of weather conditions, including lightning, as the customer looked on from the relative comfort of the cabin.

The secret spoon worked great for three years (I was a mate for Jimmy for two of these years: 2008 to 2009). The big bass had never seen anything like it, and they pounced. Years later, however, when the bunker returned due to the banning of commercial pair seining, the bass, once again enjoyed an abundance of their favorite bait—the oily, fatty menhaden—and no longer felt the need to assault a big piece of swimming metal (either that, or the fish that were susceptible to the lure were already killed). I used to joke with Jimmy years later, telling him that I'd seen his spoon on sale on the Lower East Side displayed on a blanket next to an old toaster, random DVDs, and a set of speakers. In the end, Jimmy may have the last laugh because I heard the spoons have recently been working well in Jersey.

From 2006 to 2008, the *Nicole Marie* was the busiest charter boat (next to Captain Mark) in Montauk. Jimmy George was a big, charismatic man with a lot of stories and a personality larger than life. People loved him, and they loved his spoons. He sailed twice a day and did the occasional night trip with me running the deck. I learned a lot. Though Jimmy was known for having a fiery temper, I never saw it. He was always cool under pressure, and the crazier things got, the calmer he became. Lose a 250-pound mako? No sweat, that's all part of it, he would say as we deployed the next rig. I never saw him get flustered or yell at me or any of our customers, which is no small feat. I also never saw him happy to get the "word"—when a customer starts to get sick and tells the captain they want to go in. A lot of captains rejoice when they hear this, as it's a shorter day for them. Jimmy, on the other hand, obsessed over catching world record striped bass, so he saw anything that took him away from fishing as a setback.

When Jimmy first came to Montauk, he got a lot of flak from other charter boats, mostly on the VHF radios. Out of solidarity or spite, none of the captains bought or used the secret spoon, and many mocked it. This stopped abruptly when Jimmy met them on the dock. Jimmy was a tough man from the streets of Paterson, New Jersey. He grew up fighting not because he wanted to but because he had to. I don't think the Montauk fleet was prepared to deal with Jimmy George. Most people backed down from Jimmy's dock. There were some pretty brutal confrontations.

Jimmy was not delusional, like a lot of six pack weekend warriors were. He treated fishing like a sport, and he loved it. He was in the trucking business and knew the commercial guys were in an entirely different league than him. But many sought him out for blackfish and large striped bass fishing. In addition to being funny and a great story teller, he was also an excellent diesel mechanic, which is why he found as much success as he did.

***

The *Nicole Marie* has a glowing history as one of the top boats in Montauk: five times on the front page of fishing magazines, four times on the front page of *Nor'east Saltwater* magazine, and once on the front page of *Sport Fishing* magazine. Jimmy captured the third largest American mako shark, landing at 1,030 pounds, and a 69.75-pound striped bass on his very own Secret Spoon.

I received great tips while I was working for Jimmy. I remember two $500 tips and a few $300 ones; $200 was the norm, $150 was okay, and $100 was a rarity. In 2008, Jimmy slowed from 80 trips the previous year to 40. We went offshore to the canyon a few times for tuna. I will never forget one perfect and calm night, pulling yellowfin after yellowfin. Amazing stuff! Wealthy clients would hire us a week at a time for the Martha's Vineyard Striped Bass & Bluefish Derby. I had many $2,000 weeks. Sometimes, I didn't even bother trolling the next day since the coolers were full.

***

I met Jimmy after I had just made $75 grand for my movie, *American Loser*. I moved out to Montauk shortly thereafter and tried to spend every penny as quickly as possible in pursuit of striped bass. Luckily, I didn't drink or party, otherwise the money would've only lasted one year instead of three. Montauk is a huge party town, so not drinking was the only reason I lasted as long as I did.

Not drinking allowed me to fish day and night. I had no interest in partying or girls or having a family; I was simply obsessed with catching a 60-pound striped bass. Jimmy and I were alike in this regard, and I saved a lot of money by working for him because I wouldn't be fishing on my own boat, burning gas.

Funny, now that I'm older, it would be nice to nail a 60-pound bass (which I'd have every intention of releasing, just as long as there was a yardstick and good camera aboard), but the insatiable drive is no longer there. Whether that's due to maturity, I don't know. Age makes us wiser, and I'm just not the chest pounder I once was. Looking back, the drive for the 60 pound striped bass almost seems kind of silly. I still yearn for the beautiful, crisp, clear, starry nights, the huge moons, the epic sunrises and sunsets, the alluring smell of the ocean, and the excitement of the bite. But I'm also conflicted and tormented by the environmental impact that my 15-plus years have had on the fishery. One could argue that no one alive has landed more 40-pound fish than me—not because I was that good, but because I arrived at Montauk at the greatest time in the history of striped bass and had all the time in the world to learn the trade. I often caught five fish over 40 pounds in a night; I let most of them go, and I like to think I did an adequate job of reviving and releasing them. But who knows? Fish aren't known for bouncing back too well after a fight, especially in warm water over 70 degrees. If they died and floated back to the surface, I would throw them in the boat and sell the gorgeous old mercury laden breeder for $2 a pound. The profit from the fish went back into the machine.

For me, it was all ego. I was never a good athlete and failed at a lot jobs, including a six-year stint as a standup comedian. So, hoisting an elusive and coveted 50-pound bass on the scale and getting my picture on the front of a flimsy fishing magazine made me a legend in my own mind, and in the minds of a very small and shrinking group of trophy hunters. It proved I could do something, even though, in truth, it does not take much skill. The reel does most of the work; you just need the time.

In 2003, it just so happened that I kept a small 22-foot Angler outboard at the same marina as Jimmy George. Fishing was different back then: fishermen were tight-lipped, there wasn't much Internet exposure, and no one talked to strangers on the dock (you couldn't even get a hello from most of them, even if you said one first—not a word).

There was a bench outside of the bait shop where fishermen would converse. One day, some guys were making fun of me at the dock near that bench, and Jimmy happened to be sitting there at the time. Though Jimmy was a tough guy, he hated bullies (he'd been bullied when he was a kid), and it should be noted that I had once given him a nice piece of mako steak for the barbie, which may be why he felt moved to defend me. "Why make fun of the guy," Jimmy tells the guys who'd been ragging on me. "He seems like a nice guy. He likes to fish, he spends money here, so why pick on him?"

They said I didn't know how to run a boat, and they called me a rich kid and retarded. Jimmy stopped them. "So that makes it okay to make fun of him? What if I made fun you guys?"

They had nothing to say to this.

"Look," Jimmy continued, "when I'm around, don't say anything bad about the guy."

And that was that. They stopped heckling me. In fact, most were overtly nice to me. From that day, no one said a derogatory thing about me (as far as I know), and people treated me differently on the radio. It was a real game changer. Jimmy ran into trouble, as happens in the fishing business, and left Montauk for a while. Just a few years after he left, the locals dismissed him. I was respected for a short time after Jimmy left, but over time people forgot, and I no longer had the clout of the *Nicole Marie* behind me.

Ultimately, Jimmy and I had a falling out. He accused me of going into his GPS and stealing his "numbers," something I did not do. No surprise there, falling out with a fishing friend. Happens all the time. Egos get hurt, and things fall into the abyss quickly. There is so much money and pride involved.

Chapter 13

Kind of a Total Dick

By 2005, I had mated on some top professional charter and party boats and gotten some experience and exposure to the Montauk fishing world, but far from enough. This, by the way, is very common. A guy mates on a boat one year, decides he gained enough experience, takes the test, steals some "numbers" from his former boss, buys a boat, gets his friend to sign off on sea time, and *bang*—he is technically a captain the next year.

By 2008, I was a renegade—a term used by the tight-knit Montauk charter boat community to refer to a part-time captain. Nonetheless, I ran a registered and documented legal charter boat with all the appropriate stickers and documents.

Early on, I fished mostly at night for striped bass, so none of the established daytime charter boat captains paid me much mind; I was not yet on their "radar" as the "demon of the charter boat industry," as I am now, or the "Groupon guy," even though I was posting pictures of huge striped bass on fishing websites every day and had a few customers on the cover of fishing magazines. Back then, for whatever reason, it was strictly a night bite for big bass (today, they do well in the daytime, too), and not in Montauk, for me anyway. I fished at a place near Block Island a couple miles from the now controversial Southwest Ledge. No one's allowed to fish there anymore after a congressional act made it illegal to target striped bass three miles off the coast, creating a sanctuary of sorts, but people still fish there, especially poachers from Massachusetts who see the $1,000 fine as the "price of doing business," since they can make up for that loss the next night within two hours. Anyway, don't get me going on the lack of environmental enforcement. It's not all doom and gloom for the bass fishery, and there were some arrests last year. But boats need to be seized and people need to do real prison time to protect this beautiful fish, the *Morone saxatilis*, from becoming extinct.

Those nights at Block Island, often under magnificent full moons or the equally great new moons, the stars would appear like diamonds on a jeweler's black cloth. (Wow, that's a pretty good simile, or was it too cliché? Either way, don't expect to many more of them; I'm a storyteller, not a novelist.) Anyway, I was genuinely blessed, I'd had many gorgeous nights out on Block Island sound, and I have witnessed more sunrises and epic sunsets than anyone deserves. I try to remain grateful, but that's not human nature, is it? We want more. With all the shit we go through in life, the traps we create or fall into, the very real injustices bestowed on us, it's easy to get so bogged down that we often forget the beauty we have seen and touched and smelled, and what a divine privilege it was. "Ha-la-lu-yay" (the dyslexic's way for writing hallelujah!).

Anyway, mine was always the only boat at this particular area. In fact, if look at some of my many videos on YouTube, there's never a boat in sight.

Jimmy George of the *Nicole Marie* used to fish there by day, landing many 50-pound (plus) fish on the spoon, and he'd be the only boat there (this was before people had GPS on their phones so customers could not steal coordinates as they do now). He said I could go there by myself at night, but if I told anyone about the spot (called the Pig Pen) or ever brought anyone over there, there'd be a big problem between us. I promised I would not and started going at night, by myself, and I was always the only one there. The fishing was amazing; I couldn't have been happier: no wife or kids, no real job or career. Even though I wasn't getting laid, on drugs, drinking, or smoking, at the time, I had to be one of the happiest people on earth. I would fish all night, often landing over 30 fish, many in the 40-pound class. But I had only one real obsession in life: catching the elusive 60 pounder. That's all I cared about. I had plenty of 50s (eight of which, for ego's sake alone, I weighed in officially at the Gone Fishing Marina). Looking back, I wish I'd taken a picture and thrown them all back, as restaurants that I often sold to would not take big, tough, mercury-laden fish from me.

I would keep my legal limit (at that time, it was one at 40 inches and one below) and come back through the inlet at dawn or a little after; if the tide was right, there was often a good "first light bite" that I didn't want to miss. So, with a half hour ride back to Montauk Harbor, I probably arrived at 5:30 a.m., exhausted after fishing two tides. I did not time it this way on purpose, but it always seemed to be when the fleet of charter boats were heading out. I wished them well because I know how hard it is and the commitment it takes to put together a fishing trip: picking the right boat, finding six guys that want to go and can afford $150, making sandwiches at 3 a.m., driving three hours. I have done it myself many times. I would dock my boat, have coffee with the boys at the marina, go back to the boat, ice the fish down again, make a halfhearted attempt to clean the bloodstained, rank boat. I was always bad at this—cleaning stuff. I was always about the fun and glory, but never about the maintenance, upkeep, and cleaning. This is why many customers stopped fishing with me, and why I don't have a boat today.

I never got my 60-pound striper, by the way—probably never will. I hope I don't because I will probably kill it and put it on the scale for ego's sake. I am not that delusional; I know myself.

***

My last book, *Caught*, sold about three copies online, despite some good reviews and a book signing at my mother's house in Florida. I have no shame about this—I did not ask her to do it, but I didn't tell her not to, either. Her poor friends, many of whom had children my age who were successful lawyers and doctors, who were now forced to attend the book signing of their friend's 45-year-old, smelly, learning disabled, wayward son who unabashedly confesses in its pages to all kinds of crimes against the environment, and to selling mercury-laden fish to seedy Long Island restaurants.

By the time the high-end guests with pursed lips and, for the most part, fake smiles handed their book for me to sign, my mother had already collected their cash or check, and they could barely make eye contact with me. There must have been some heavy eye rolling when they received my mom's invitation for her the book signing party , but because my stepfather was, at one time, a powerful executive and grand marshal of the Saint Patrick's Day parade, and both were fun, lovable, hardworking people, and the food was catered, guests came in droves. One book signing on the top of my mom's building in Palm Beach had been attended by 300 people, and you can bet your ass that every one of them bought a copy of my book because my mom was there to jam it down their throats. God forbid anyone try to duck out of the party without buying the book (as some did, I'm sure)—my mom would chase them down to their cars. If they said they forgot their checkbook (which they often did; they had all the lines), she pulled out and handed them a ready-made self-addressed, stamped envelope, along with a copy of my book; and if they didn't send the check to pay for it, she would call or confront them on the tennis court in front of their entire country club to shame them into buying the book, gosh darnit!

In the book, I had confessed not to being a poacher (someone who takes over his legal limit) but a horrific bootlegger of fish. It is against the law to sell fish without a food license, which I did not have. The restaurants in Long Island and New York City that I illegally sold to loved just about any fish I had that was under 30 pounds (they didn't want the big girls, so I'd give the inedible old fish to the dockhands and mechanics or an unsuspecting thrilled tourist who happened to be at the dock).

***

While generally good natured, I was often a terrible, belligerent, nasty captain when I knew I had to produce. I suppose I was desperate for the customer to catch huge fish. "Guaranteed 40-pound fish or your charter is free," I had advertised in all the magazines. Other captains mocked my naivety—they all thought I was a joke. I had to prove them wrong, and I did time and time again. I never gave back a dime (unless it was on one of the many Coast Guard rescues).

To achieve this goal, however, I was often short with customers. I was always tired from lack of sleep, but that's not the reason. I had to be tough and stern; I had to yell. Most, certainly not all, charter boat captains, especially trophy bass guys, are dicks. There are, of course, exceptions. Skip from the *Adios* comes to mind, as does Jimmy George; great dispositions, these captains had—never flustered, or never appeared to be. You'd hear it all the time: "That captain was kind of a total dick!" I understand this; because of factors like tide and wind, there is often no time to be nice. Especially back then in Montauk, when fishing was not as good (not Block Island at the Pig Pen, where, per Jimmy George's orders, I had not brought any people to fish . . . yet; customers were wondering where the fish were coming from, that's for sure, and I was starting to leak; I have a big mouth, always got me into trouble), you knew that when the bite was on, it could turn off just as fast. And one drunk guy; one spaced out, overconfident, OxyContin-addicted moron; one tangle, snarl, or bird's nest created by a customer could be the difference between being the talk of the dock and being skunked.

More importantly, having to give money back for not landing the customer's guaranteed 40-pound bass was not an option. If they didn't catch it, they'd blame you and only you, and they would spread the word.

So, of course I was a dick! I'd tell my customers not to talk. I would berate them, tell them if they wanted to catch a big fish, forget about everything they'd ever learned or knew or thought they knew about fishing and listen to me, which was kind of true. Bass fishing and the tides on Long Island Sound are all I know in life. I know nothing about 401k plans, I'll leave that to the financial analysts. If I had the same wealth of information and knowledge about the stock market as I do about tides on the Block Island Sound, I would be rich (by the way, most guys I yelled at were blue-collar tough guys that could kick the shit out of me on land, but they wanted to catch, so they obeyed me out there; I never had a mutiny or even a well-deserved "fuck you"). If I felt a 40-pounder was on the line and the customer was doing a bad job reeling it in, or the fish was pulling to a rock pile that would instantly cut the line, or the fish was getting under the boat near the prop and the customer couldn't stop it, or there was a buoy coming up, or another boat was getting close (in Montauk, there are often 50 boats hitting the same spots, so it's easy to get cut off—not often, but it happens), I would yank the rod from the customer's hands halfway through the fight to ensure that the fish got on in the boat. Looking back, I regret doing that. That should never happen. Never take a rod from a customer's hand; they're paying to fish, for Christ's sake! Some charter captains, especially egotistical striped bass guys, really can be total dicks.

Finally, and I guess inevitably, I brought some customers over to Jimmy George's secret spot, the Pig Pen near Block Island, where he'd asked me never to bring anyone. People started following me at night over there, 13 miles from Montauk Harbor. I have a big mouth. Soon, the entire fleet—not only from Montauk, but Connecticut, Rhode Island, and even Orient Point descended on the area. The charter boats were there in the daytime, too, coming out to what Jimmy and I had once to ourselves.

After that, Jimmy literally tied to kill me. It was very scary and very real. I had to leave Montauk for three weeks, hiding in one room of my apartment with my neighbor's gun, I shit you not!

***

When I really think about what I've done in my life, where striped bass fishing has taken me, I want to fall on a knife. Most of all because business is cyclical. Because there is a dollar value on every fish and a demand for it, and every time stocks get wiped out again in the name of commerce, there's a necessary recovery period. Big fish are not sustainable. They take 15 years to mature. I imagine in 2025, people won't even try for them. Hopefully, there will be another recovery, but who knows? I'm not banking on it. There was a crash in the mid and late nineteenth century—the 1850s and the 1880s. According to Dick Russell's *Striper Wars*, where he painstakingly documents the striped bass's history in America, it always happens abruptly; there were plenty of fish, and then there were none.

In 2008, I did, perhaps, 16 to 20 legitimate, paid, state documented trips with real customers (not my retarded friends who would only pay me 20 bucks, take all the fish, never help clean the boat, and then call me on their drive home to complain about the traffic). My price was low—from $200 to $450; some say it was too cheap, and that it degraded the fleet. I would sometimes take one guy for $150 for a five-hour half day. I would sell all the fish I caught, so it kind of made it worthwhile.

Too cheap? Anyone who said so has never seen the filthy operation I run. My boat was a 1998 33-foot Vector Hydra-Sport that was, at one point way before I owned it, a sleek and gorgeous fishing boat that was undoubtedly the star of the 1998 boat show circuit, capable of hitting 45 knots; the one drawback is it might have been a little too *Miami Vice*-ish. But under my command, the boat had fallen into disrepair and was now a heinous, rank, vomit and bloodstained, appallingly unorganized vessel. It was called *Second Choice Charters* for fuck's sake. I named it that for a reason. What did you expect? How much was I supposed to charge? Half of my customers left with hooks in their asses.

What was a fair price? All my poles and reels were old and outdated, and many were missing eyes and even tips. On a particularly good day, both engines would be working and, if we were lucky, one of the three debris-clogged bilge pumps that drained the porous hull might click on from time to time.

But I have learned something about fishing: If the weather's good and the rods are bent and the fish are coming over the deck, everyone has a blast, even if your boat's a shit tub. Conversely, if you're on a spotless, odor free, brand new 300 Grady-White and you're not catching a damn thing, it sucks! But yes; all things equal, better a clean boat than a dirty one. Although clean freaks terrify me for some reasons, it's better to fish with a clean freak than a slob. If the fishing was good, I would usually keep my customers out longer because, back then, in most cases, I did not have a second trip.

It was great at first. I was anonymous, a nobody—no one knew who I was. I put a toe in the water, I hung a little benign shingle on a pylon next to my boat sheepishly announcing my operation, *Second Choice Charters*. I felt that with this innocuous name, the formable tight-knit charter boat community would not feel threatened by me. I mean, if *Second Choice Charters* was a threat to your business, you really could not have much of a business to begin with.

*

One more quick note: If you want to get in the charter game, do yourself a favor: Tell your customers that your head (what we boatmen call the toilet on our vessels) is broken. Do not let them shit in the head. Make them use a bucket! By the way, a bucket is a great thing to shit into. You get a much better spread. It's probably more sanitary too.

Not only do people puke, but they shit. Especially little kids—no matter how short the trip is, if you have a toilet on board, those little fuckers will try to shit in it, and their metro fathers and mothers will go along with it. For this reason, I pulled the entire head out of my boat. One time, I had an eight-year-old boy—a snotty, whiny motherfucker—on a three-hour porgy trip who insisted he had to take a shit. I showed him the makeshift bathroom and told him to shit into the bucket and call me when he was done so I could dump it overboard. Well, when he called me back, I looked, but there was nothing in the bucket. I figured he didn't have to shit, after all. But then, a week or so later, I started to smell something pungent coming from where the head once was. There was a hole where the head used to be, and, apparently, this little punk dumped the bucket of shit down the hole. I tried bleach and disinfectant, but no amount of anything worked. I probably have a tumor growing inside me from the amount of cleaner I inhaled to remove the stench, but I could never get the odor out. I sold the boat to a friend, and he says to this day, when there is no wind, it still reeks.

Part Three

Chapter 14

What is Groupon and How Does It Work?

As you may know—come on, it's okay to admit you use it—Groupon is an online, volume-based discount service. Millions of customers venture the site every day in search of a good deal on all kinds of goods and services: movies, haircuts, bowling, splat ball, concerts, trips to national parks, bike rentals. You name it, they probably have it. And it doesn't stop there.

Groupon is willing to do business with pretty much anyone. I am a case in point. I've had five Coast Guard rescues and more citations over 10 years than I care to count. I'm also involved in two lawsuits from horrified/mystified customers who were simply looking for a nice time on the water with their friends. Instead, when some heavy seas unexpectedly arrived, they were told that the ship was sinking, commanded to put on life preservers, forced to remain in the engine room, and handed a five-gallon bucket with which they had to bail endless amounts of intruding water for two hours—puking the entire time—as we waited for the Coast Guard to come.

One poor, good-natured, young woman was trapped in my filthy makeshift bathroom for an hour. This was my first year doing Groupon, so I rarely had women aboard. I was not prepared. My "bathroom" was, in fact, a disgusting red five-gallon bucket containing a splash of water and bleach behind a sliding door under the steering center console. To my credit, the bucket had an old, peeling toilet seat precariously duct taped on top. Apparently, the door had gotten stuck while she was down there, and she couldn't open it, so she was basically trapped in a chamber of horrors. The fishing was excellent, so all her friends and I forgot about her. When we finally realized she was missing, I found her down there, sobbing, covered in shit and puke. I had to clean this poor woman off with a hose. She was completely humiliated; I'd have sued if I was her, too. Imagine if that happened to you or your date in a restaurant?

It may come as no surprise that I have to settle a lot of stuff in court. I also have all negative reviews on Yelp and Groupon, citing my abusive language and general smelliness. But still, if you look up deep sea fishing in Montauk on Groupon, there you will find me: *Second Choice Charters*.

*

On Groupon, there are all kinds of businesses, from nail salons to chiropractors to amusement parks, and there is no accountability. Groupon did not even ask to see my captain's license! If they check into these places at all, it is very superficial. Like, they may click on a website if one is provided. But that's it. They don't ask for tax returns or insurance documents or anything. Even though they take half the money, they clearly state that the owners are responsible and liable for their product or service. And, of course, they emphasize: Buyer beware.

On the upside, if you're a merchant who needs more business, Groupon can likely rustle you up some. Because, at 3 million views a day, they are the gateway to the customers in your area who don't yet know you even exist. And before you degrade Groupon customers and dismiss them as low-class, cheapskate opportunists looking for great deals—file that underisn't everyone?—you'd be surprised at the cars some of these Groupon customers pull up in. Everyone I had on my trips were good people who tipped well. Groupon designed a way to take a huge 50 percent cut, and then mark the asking price so far down that customers simply can't resist biting. And they offer discounts on top of this.

Most say that Groupon is not really good for fishing trips because you can only take so many people out on a boat. This is true—Groupon works if, say, you own a 200-seat steakhouse and you're only getting 100 seats filled on a Saturday night, and you don't want your place to look half empty. Then, Groupon is for you. "Dinner for two: $39! Save 70 percent!" Groupon's also good for Broadway shows. Say your reviews were okay but not great, and you're hanging by a thread trying to keep doors open while you watch lines stretch around the block for *Hamilton*.

Groupon worked for me. Simple formula: I wasn't sailing much; I had very few paying customers; I joined Groupon; and now, I was busy.

*

Here's how it works.

Groupon asks how much your average dinner for two is. Say it's $75. Groupon will cut that price in half and advertise the deal on their site: "Dinner for two: $37.99!" And then, they take half of that (Groupon may discount on top of this, too, like if you buy in the next hour, take another 20 percent off, then another discount that on top *if* you buy that day). So, you only get a little over $18 per sale. Sounds terrible, but wait! What if they order drinks? What if they come back and bring their friends the next week? What if they leave a huge tip? Your place is empty, you've got to do something. On the other hand, they will design a page for you with a link to your website. So basically, you're making jack shit—a little over $15 a sale—but at least your establishment is full. And if, for example with a Broadway play, you sell 300 seats for $15, that's $4,500 you wouldn't have had.

This formula, however, does not translate well to charter fishing. Maybe large party boats that need volume, but not six pack boats where you're selling six rather than 100 tickets. But somehow, it worked for me; I stayed in local waters, caught fish, and got great tips. How did I get great tips? Often, I would beg. "Please, Groupon is taking half, you've got to help me."

I also discovered a loophole on Groupon that I would take advantage of. First, I would put a link to my website on my Groupon page. Next, I added a note that said, "Call the captain directly three weeks ahead for availability; reservations only." Then, when the calls came in, I would squeeze out Groupon. I'd tell customers that if they worked with me directly rather than purchasing the Groupon, I'd not only take another $50 off, but I would give them a better trip—burn more gas, use better bait, etc. I was essentially using the Groupon platform to attract the customer, and then pushing them out of the sale. Unethical? Perhaps. But it was a way to even it out because, when people did buy vouchers from Groupon, I'd only make $179 off the sale, and that didn't make sense. All their discounting was killing my business. And for me, it was worth it. Even if I dropped my price to $250, I'd sometimes get a $150 or $200 tip if the fishing was good. Better than being tied up at the dock.

Consequently, in 2017, I was the busiest boat in Montauk. I fished around the clock and logged 150 trip report forms with the Department of Environmental Conservation. I burned through three mates, all of whom were making a minimum of $1,200 a week (Thursday to Sunday). They just couldn't take the relentless pace and hours my boat required.

Chapter 15

Customers Will Drive You Crazy

Anyway, back to chit chat. I have found that a lot people, while on the boat, really don't want to know the answers to the questions they're asking. One time, a guy with a big toothy grin asked me at least 12 times how many miles Block Island Sound was from Montauk. I told him 10 times: about 15 miles. Finally, when he asked again, I was like, "Do you really want to know the answer to this question?"

I think most guides or charter boat captains would rather have an expert fisherman or a brand new fisherman—preferably a kid who learns fast—than an intermediate fisherman; those kinds of guys know a little, but they think they know everything, which is problematic. "We should be fishing over there with those boats." "Why can't we go to Block?" "I'm going to let some more line out and fish with my shitty fluke pole." A lot of times I'll say to these guys, "Listen, just for today, throw out everything you have learned about fishing. If you want to catch big bass, or catch any fish for that matter, listen and do what I say." I often preface this with a practiced look that says "striped bass is all I know."

It is not a tough sport. Really any idiot with a boat and GPS and a lot of time on their hands can learn how to catch fish consistently. Unfortunately for the fishery that I happened upon during its zenith in 2002, when the waters from early May to November were infested with striped bass, I had all the time in the world to fish, and I did so 100 nights a year for 15 years. I'm saying this with no ego; in fact, I'm a little ashamed by it. Probably no man alive has caught more 40-pound fish than me (I just hit the right time history, egomaniac collided), but it takes time to learn how to feel for the bottom and avoid snagging it on every drift, or how to set the hook, or how to release the fish properly so it lives.

Also, this may sound simple, but you have to know the tides. This is critical. I'm always surprised by how many people don't understand how important this is. The only things I know for certain in life are the tides in Block Island Sound. I know when the fish will bite, when they'll move from one side of a boulder to the other. If you asked me what the tide will be doing off Montauk Point in February at 12 or 10 p.m. in 2020, I could tell you in about two minutes. I have a formula. Usually, on a full moon, the tide starts at Montauk Point at 5:20 p.m. and 5:20 a.m. So, I start there. Now, I know the tide on the next day will start at 5:40 a.m. Then, at 6:10 a.m. on the next. Then at 7 a.m. And so on. Factoring in that the moon grows weaker and the slack tides grow longer during that time, I know the fish won't bite. I can go on and on about the tides and bass.

*

Once, I had a nice group for an afternoon trip. I still had to retie all the lines, and quickly, too, because the bite was on and there was no time to waste. I quickly asked one woman if she could drive the boat straight out, pointing to the ocean. I knew she had no experience, but all she had to do was drive straight toward the ocean; there was no other option. The jetties announcing Montauk Harbor were straight, creating perfect borders, and it was the afternoon, so there wasn't much boat traffic.

My line of thinking was this: She probably didn't drive, but most young people have played computer games, and on computer games, you know, if you hit the wall, you crash. Right? Game over—or at least you lose points. After only about two minutes, as I was tying knots and setting up polls, I looked up and saw that she was heading right into the rock jetty! None of her friends said anything; they just laughed, if I recall. Ten more seconds, and we would've crashed.

*

You meet some interesting people in the charter boat fishing business. One time, I had a group of five guys; we'd gotten out a little late, so the fishing was slow on the incoming tide and the bite was off. In other words: no fish. So, I told them that if we waited through slack for about an hour, the fish might turn on. They agreed to give it a shot, and we just sat there in the slack tide. Early in the day, one of them told me they were all in the industrial waste management business. I was pretty bored, so I asked them to tell me more about their business. Turned out, they worked for the hazmat union—the union that does toxic cleanups—and these five guys were part of that union's subgroup that did the particularly brutal high-profile cleanups. They got paid $30 bucks an hour. No one wanted the job, they told me, and most can't handle it. They had no problem furnishing me with the specific details.

So, here is what their group would do:

Whenever someone, for instance, jumped off an apartment building, splattering 6th Avenue, they'd be called in to clean up whatever was left over. In one high-profile case, a woman jumped of a Marriott balcony and landed on the promenade, her body shattered into tiny parts from the impact. It was all captured on their surveillance cameras, and these guys were called in with the police to go over the footage. In another particularly gruesome case, a woman who was running to catch a crowded elevator slipped, skidded head first, and stopped with half of her body in the elevator, half out. The doors shut on her, and the elevator started moving up. Again, the whole thing was caught on the elevator's camera, and the guys had to watch as everyone, in horror, pressed all the alarms and desperately tried prying the doors open to no avail. When the elevator hit the second floor, the shrieking lady's body exploded. Again and again, I was mesmerized by what these guys saw on a daily basis.

The good news: When the tide turned, these guys went out and caught two big striped bass. They were thrilled and gave me a nice tip.

Chapter 16

Conversations on Boats

Slack tide, dead fishing, or no fish biting often lead to conversation. You get know the people you share the water with. Sometimes, the conversation comes naturally, or at least it's not forced. I hate forced conversation; we all do. You know the guy's bored and uncomfortable when he launches into a series of rapid-fire, directionless questions. Just nervous energy, these questions. They're not intrusive, but they are annoying.

I like to catch fish. If we're out there to catch fish, and we're not catching fish, no one is having fun! And I am pissed. So, I don't want to chitchat about how some guy's pension eligibility is coming up in a year. For some reason, fisherman love talking about their pensions, and Medicare, and 401k accounts. I guess because I don't have any of this stuff, I feel like falling on a knife whenever that conversation comes up. I'd rather hear someone talk about how he sucked a cock behind a dumpster at the 7-11 for a six pack than listen to some school teacher or fireman drone on about his fucking pension. Then, they start in on me. How do I pay for the slip at the marina? What's the maintenance on the condo my mom bought for me? I have perfected the curt, blunt, one-word answer in a clear non-conversational tone that eventually makes the guy stop asking questions. If I ever get a boat again, I'll put up a sign that says, "Talking is not at all necessary when fishing."

*

There's kind of a Murphy's Law at work on the water. The times you really need to catch a fish for a customer—when it is absolutely essential—for whatever reason (usually the wind), it simply doesn't happen. It can be when a member of the New York Yankees is on board (this happened to a friend, and they didn't catch one fish; the day before, they had seven), or a kid in a wheelchair, or a person with terminal cancer who just wants one more shot at a big bass.

For instance, I once had Chad Smith from the Red Hot Chili Peppers on my boat with a few of his friends from Los Angeles—they were unfortunate enough to win my trip at a black tie auction fundraiser. Of course, the seas were rough as hell that day, the wind against the tide was blowing 15 to 20 knots for most of the morning. I met them at the dock, and though I hated to, I wanted the photo op with Chad holding a big fish. So, in good conscience, I advised them to reschedule because of the poor conditions (I don't know why I didn't call the night before; I guess the wind hadn't been forecasted). But (possibly like Caroline Bessette-Kennedy was when she convinced John to fly to Martha's Vineyard on that fateful foggy night) they were excited to be there, and they couldn't reschedule since Chad's 80-year-old dad was with them. They claimed they were tough and demanded that we go. I told them it was too rough to fish for big bass in the rips and that the wind would be against the tide all morning. So, we went out in the big Vector, which could handle any sea. I took them offshore to calmer waters, and they did catch some small sea bass and one keeper fluke, but not the coveted Striper that everyone wants in Montauk. I may have jinxed the trip because, on the outside chance that we didn't catch a striper,

I saved one that I'd caught the night before, so at least I would have one for the photo shoot. The picture is still on the website.

*

After I gave away the Bertram for $1,000 dollars, I tried to just mate on friends' boats for a while. I filled in on a party boat a few times and made a little bit of money as a charter boat broker, though that's more trouble than it's worth: trying to put together parties, checking the weather, dealing with other captains' egos.

I needed to get out on my own again, so I looked around for used, smaller, more manageable boats. With my scant $2,500 budget, I found a 1974 30v Wellcraft with a newer four-stroke 140 horsepower Suzuki engine. Of course, it was a Ray Hunt deep-V design.

This little boat ran great (see pictures). I piled a lot of people on that thing. The problem was that it wasn't self-bailing (most boats were not back then), and there was a crack in the splash well, so sea water leaked into the bilge. It was a constant battle to keep the water out. I kept going through bilge pumps and had some crazy white-water rides home.

Ultimately, that little boat sank at the dock in November 2019. At first, I was excited because I had taken out insurance, but then I checked and found out it had lapsed the month before. It cost a fortune to have it pulled out of the water and hauled to the dump. But in the end, I'm glad it sank at the dock and not out in the rips with people on board. I am now walking dogs and trying to make a living at that (it's really picking up . . . get it?). An honest day's work for an honest day's pay, something that has always eluded me.

Chapter 17

And Then They All Puked!

A word on puking.

On your average charter, one out of six customers will puke, and often on remarkably calm days, too. Even if they remember to take their Dramamine, passengers always seem to take it too late; I tell them to take it the night before, or at least an hour before they jump on the boat, but most don't. Only when they start to feel queasy do they poke around for their Dramamine. I don't discourage them from doing so, in case the possible, though highly unlikely, placebo effect kicks in, but in the majority of cases, they're goners.

The first sign that someone's going to puke is silence. They go from asking a hundred questions to not saying a word. I don't even have to ask; I know they are sick and they're not going to pull out of it. Few recover until they're back on land. Sometimes, sick passengers give me the word to head back to land. But oftentimes, they'll stay out, and I've seen people puke and pull fish at the same time. You've got to love that drive.

On rough days, of course, the rate of puking increases. It's more like three out of six, and it can quickly escalate to six out of six. The guys, every one of them, violently puked for two to three hours straight—sheer misery. Usually, the guy that put the trip together fishes more than his friend, since he's paying for it. So he generally won't want to go home, no matter how sick his friends are.

Recovery is also virtually impossible on the water. Sure, after someone pukes, people offer the obligatory hopeful statements—even I do—knowing full well that this poor son of a bitch won't recover until his feet hit the dock. Then, it disappears instantly, which is the only upside to seasickness.

*

Everyone thinks they have the antidote to seasickness. "You should eat bread," they'll say. Or "Try staring at an object, it will center you. Like the lighthouse. Look at the lighthouse. Look at the lighthouse!" It never works. I hear it all the time, but the puking continues. Now, don't get me wrong, I'm a nice guy. I truly feel their pain. They came out for a nice time, drove for hours, spent a lot of money, looked forward to the trip, and now look: misery!

The worst is fog. In fog, people lose their reference point. We get a lot of fog in Montauk in May and June, at least every other day—fog and a rocky outgoing tide. In conditions like these, you don't just get one person puking, you most likely getting all six customers puking.

What is hard to take . . . and interesting and funny . . . is that they paid for this. Sure, people get chemo and get sick, which sucks, but they're doing it to survive and they know a bad time is coming. These people, however, came out on my boat thinking they were going to have a good time at sea! Not only did they not have a good time (that happens), but they had a remarkably bad time—which is far worse than just puking.

And what makes the awful reality of puking even worse is the very real fact that no one, including spouses, gives a shit! On the contrary, they think it's funny or, at the very least, amusing—and here I go, giggling right now as I remember some people puking over the side of my boat. Even the most stoic, serious mothers with two kids on the boat will crack a smile as her husband violently hurls off the bow. And I can't help wondering: Why is that? If he had the flu, people would be concerned. But on a boat, we laugh or mock or don't give a shit. And generally, very few of them ask to go back to land early, especially the guy who's paying for the trip; he especially does not want to.

After the laughter subsides, the miserable soul is often abandoned. His body lifeless, head hanging listlessly over the corner of the boat or resting against the hard fiberglass gunnel. Especially if the fishing is good, people will fish right over this poor, sick bastard. They'll eat sandwiches right over them, crumbs landing on the victim's green face. The person is so vulnerable; no matter how strong or well-built someone is—he may be able squat 600 and bench 450—when you're nauseous, you're as helpless as a newborn deer. If you wanted to go take their wallet, and then piss on them, they couldn't do a damn thing no matter how big they are. Until they hit the dock, that is.

Once on the *Nicole Marie*, a customer offered Jimmy $600 to take them near shore so they could swim in. Jimmy would not because the bite was good, and it was illegal.

*

As I said earlier, my boats were particularly designed to induce nausea.

The worst puking fest I ever witnessed was when four giant men—every one of them over 400 pounds—from Maryland chartered me out. They had heard about me and sought me out, which is the best way to do business; when they come to you, you have the leverage. They knew the odds of catching a trophy fish were high with me.

We hit Montauk Point first, then we drifted for a while and picked up one or two nice 30-pound bass before the bite slowed down. I knew it was over, but they'd had some action, and, in hindsight, I should have dragged the trip out in local waters, driven home slowly, and gotten paid. Hey, I wish every customer I ever had caught fish, but not every day is Christmas, either. But that's not what I did. Instead, I told them my friend had just landed a 65-pound bass over on my spot (the Pig Pen) near Block Island on a boat called the *Caprice* run by Captain Bob Stork. The night before, I'd seen that he had headed over their again. I warned the customers that it would be rougher over there because the southwest wind tends to make the waves stand up more over there.

They were, of course, up for it. Evidently, they all stopped listening after I mentioned the 65 pounder. I got us to the place in a half hour, and the waves were big. It was fishable, but there was a hard, rocky drift. One guy puked as soon as we stopped. I hadn't baited a single hook before the rest of these fat bastards followed suit. One guy tried to escape to the cabin, only to come out running minutes later saying, "Oh god! Oh god!" and then violently puking over the side. The guy who had paid for the trip wanted to stay out, so the other three just rolled around and puked. At one point, they no longer had the energy to pick their heads up and puke over the side, so they just puked on themselves and on each other—and, of course, all over the deck. Picture it for a moment: three huge, 400-pound men, on a small, 26-foot boat, puking all over each other.

From that time until we pulled up to the dock, no one spoke. I asked the guy the next day to send a picture of the fish he'd caught. All he sent was a sad picture of a fish deck, with no people in this picture. Those poor guys will never, ever forget that trip.

Chapter 18

Tipping the Scales

I simply couldn't keep up with all the Groupon calls I was getting. I did not anticipate this much business when I clicked on the website and signed up for the merchant service. Nor did I know it would infuriate the local charter boats—let me just clarify that I adored the charter boat industry.

I remember at night, I would often go out and just look at the boats: *Hooker, Adios, Blue Fin IV*. All those gorgeous, custom, downeaster fishing boats. Those girls gave a lot of people a lot of fun and fish. I also remember some not so aesthetically appealing boats. The *Obsession*, for instance, which was a commercial fishing boat that would catch bass at night; that one was not a great boat, cosmetically speaking, but it provided a lot of happiness for people. Rodger Brevet (the *Obsession*'s captain) was probably the best bottom fisherman around. His business was always steady, and his customers were always happy.

Because of Groupon, the community that I adored and envied now hated me. They called me a loser and a gypsy all over town, on Facebook, and even over the VHF radio, which I had to keep turned down so my customers didn't hear. I still had plenty of customers—so many that I was sailing twice every day with them, filling coolers with fish and documenting the trips online with pictures of happy customers. I didn't understand why using Groupon for my charter was so taboo in Montauk. Yes, I would take a huge financial hit, but wasn't that better than not sailing at all? Also, what about repeat business? What about introducing trophy fishing to a new demographic? I couldn't see what the problem was at the time, but when I got wind of all the complaints, I suspended the Groupon service.

I respected those guys, and wanted the best for them. The Montauk charter boat community is a noble, but fading industry for many reasons: traffic, fishing regulations, and the fact that most kids want to play video games instead of go fishing has a lot to do with it. But I also think online dating really killed it because, now, the average Joe can get a date if he clicks on enough profiles. Twenty years ago, there was no online dating, so people spent their money on fishing. On a somewhat related note: Today, to take girl out, you each have to have two glasses of wine—that's $60 right there.

I had stooped too low by crossing over to Groupon. All the captains were united on this front. I got it; they felt I was devaluing the business and undercutting their rates. But my boat, relatively speaking, was a piece of shit. While they had their gorgeous custom downeasters, the name of my little outfit was *Second Choice Charters*, for fuck's sake! I didn't even use a mate, so even without Groupon, how could I charge the same rate as the big boats? Point is: If I was a threat to anyone's business, then they really did not have one. Imagine being in the hot dog business and saying, "Ahhh we're losing business to a company that calls itself Second Choice Hot Dogs."

The Montauk fleet had much bigger problems than me: no highway to allow customers to pass the horrific "trade parade" that was Hamptons' traffic; punitive fishing regulations; an overall decline in people that want to fish. Fishing—like golf, hunting, and splat ball—are all dramatically down. Montauk's impending demise has had nothing to do with *Second Choice Charters*.

Still, many captains saw me as the enemy. On one level, I really didn't care because I was making money and catching fish. I also had some pretty devoted friends, like Jimmy George. The other boats would talk about me over the VHF radio, and they would get downright nasty at times. It didn't bother me, really. I was a renegade charter boat, and I was a little crazy, but I was happy. Fishing was great, and I was filling coolers and making people happy. I had fished with some people for years, and they'd come up and hug me after the trips…up until 2019, when the shit hit the fan. I got so in over my head with customers that I couldn't even keep up on the basic maintenance and service my boat needed. Soon, countless mechanical problems cropped up, and I had neither the knowledge nor ability to fix them.

Before all this, I often helped the charter boat fleet, for which no one will ever give me credit. I'd frequently double-book Groupon clients, then send one of the customers to another established charter boat, and I would pay the difference out of my own pocket (double-booking is something that should never happen once; I did it three or four times, but I always found customers other boats to go on, and I did right by the customers—but logistically, it was a nightmare.). Since I always caught a lot fish, they'd usually want to come back. I brought a lot of new fishermen to the area (or fishermen who had not cast their line in years and wanted to re-explore it), something Montauk desperately needs. We always need new blood. Customers would call me, and I would say I was booked but that they should try this or that other boat; I must have redirected at least 15 paying customers to established boats, never asking for a finder's fee. I did that because it was good for the harbor—good for Montauk.

A lot of people have preconceived notions of the profile of a Groupon member. In my experience, they were all nice. Most had cool careers. One of them was even a Harvard graduate. And, most importantly, all of them tipped well—*that*, by the way, was how you made money on Groupon. One observation I had about Groupon—and please understand, I don't want to offend anyone, but it really is important to note due to the nature of the business and, especially, when putting a charter boat trip together—the website had a tendency of drawing a slightly larger physical demographic. Or, more simply: there were a lot fat bastards on Groupon. Can I say that?

Many businesses on Groupon might not need this kind of information from their customers, but, as a charter boat captain, I truly needed to know if someone was obese or in a wheelchair. I had different docking and pickup options for folks with these kinds of needs. Often, they'd need tamps and a lift and people helping them on. If I hadn't had a chance to ask my customers earlier, I would call them at 5 a.m., when the charter was either just arriving or sitting in the parking lot getting ready, and sheepishly ask the person who set the trip up if there was anyone over 400 pounds in the group. Many times, they'd reply, "400 pounds, you say? Hold on . . . *Hey, Joey, the captain wants to know, what are you tipping the scales at, these days?*" I would say for about half of my Groupon customers, the answer would be yes.

A few trips, I had four people who were each over 300 pounds. I remember once asking a guy standing next to me what he thought the guy in the front of the boat weighed, and he said, "I don't know, but I'm 260." I was struck by this; compared to the other guy, the guy I had asked looked average. Today, 260 pounds is an acceptable weight for a man. Don't believe me? Go to a water park in Florida.

*

Thanks to Groupon, and Groupon only, I was busy in 2016. I was, however, falling behind. I had no steady mate, and I just couldn't do it all: pull into the dock from my morning trip, clean the fish, clean the boat, get paid, take pictures. I've never been good at delegating. If I found a customer who'd had a good time and had driven a boat before and was not puking at the time (no matter what boat you're on, no matter how clean, there's always someone puking; that's just the way it is), I would ask him to drive the boat while I cleaned the fish and retied the lines on the way back in. I'd point to the lighthouse and say, "Head for that and try not to hit anything," and then I'd go about my business (I don't recommend this; while it may seem like a good idea at the time, I guarantee that if there's a lobster pot anywhere in sight, like a moth to a flame, that motherfucker will hit it).

So, I was getting by, but I was flying by the seat of my pants. My boat was always blood stained, which is actually good, but it also stank, omitting ungodly odors. I never cleaned the bathroom, so I was getting complaints both on Groupon and Yelp. These complaints are still there, etched permanently in cyberspace. The rods were tangled, disheveled, and unprepared. In some cases, the guides were broken or missing completely. When customers complained, I would simply say that the upper guide was overrated, and it is. In fact, you can even get a fish on a pole that's missing two guides from its tip as long as there is no sharp metal fraying the line. Of course, since my company was called *Second Choice Charters*, I had to make sure it was living up to its name.

Still, one guy kept going on the radio and saying that I was ruining his business. I kept thinking, "What a fucking moron." Here I was with a piece-of-shit 1974 boat with one engine, and *I'm* the one ruining *his* business?

One guy on a popular party boat was constantly attacking me on Facebook. He acted like I had killed his newborn. Some guys wrote, "Well, *Second Choice Charters* is making Montauk look bad by putting out a substandard product." Look bad? Substandard product? I was hanging keeper makos and stripers and eight-pound fluke every trip and hitting my limit of huge sea bass, all of which I was posting on Facebook and noreast.com (a popular, if dwindling, fishing website). So yes, I was making them look bad. That's the honest truth of it.

During this time, I was happy. I had achieved my dream: I was a legit charter boat captain. I had my captain's license, and my boat was registered with NY state, and I kept my charter boat permit proudly displayed in my cabin. While not embraced by the other chart boats, I felt like a player. I would sell extra fish that customers did not want to restaurants. The restaurants, in turn (aside from cash), gave me food credit. I would bring relatively big groups of friends in, and they would drink and eat and chip in $20 bucks each for dessert. The chef or owner would come shake my hand. They called me the fish guy!

I remember driving through Montauk on a nice sunny day on my way to sell a cooler of fish I had caught the night before, thinking that this was the coolest lifestyle there was, even better than being a famous actor (who wants to memorize lines and stay in trailers all day?). I, on the other hand, got to fish all night on the gorgeous Block Island Sound. What could possibly trump a life like this?

Chapter 19

ADD medication and fishing

I believe that ADD medication is severely over-prescribed and can be dangerous. It is also an artificial crutch, just like steroids in baseball. I feel bad for kids who are put on it, however I was also in special ed for my entire school life, K-12, until I miraculously got into Hobart.

My learning disability? Well I have a horrible time, always have, with executive functions such as organization and spelling. Significant drawbacks and side affects aside, these drugs help a lot in these areas. How they work is they release a neuro transmitter, dopamine, from you brain, allowing you to get more done and more efficiently. Most of the more effective drugs are Amphetamine based, so there is a high, but not a nice one—there is some euphoria, but it's mostly a jittery weird high. Most normal well adjusted adults you give an Adderall tablet to would count the minutes until it wears off.

I'm so jealous of people who have dopamine. Dopamine is the neurotransmitter that allows people to function; it helps with motor skills, organization, and attention to detail, according to a NYU neurologist. In college, I did so many drugs (specifically E) that I wiped out a lot of dopamine. That's not good because dopamine sustains happiness and helps regulate impulsivity and executive functions.

People with ADHD are a little light on dopamine. Most functional people already have a steady stream of dopamine coursing through their brain and down their spinal cord. People with a robust supply of dopamine generally have good posture, executive function (ability to organize), can and do pull up their fly and tie their shoes, do not lay around listless, drooling on a pillow, and getting nothing done. They don't crave carbohydrates and sugar as much. So when the doctor suggested I go on it, I said why not. Wasn't I entitled to a blast of dopamine? (The answer is no, by the way. I'm a stupid old burnout. If you've used them all up, you've used them all up, and you're not entitled to a new batch of Dopamine, in my opinion.)

Thanks to Groupon, although I was remarkably busy with charters, which was good, I was also falling behind with cleaning and screwing up scheduling by double-booking. And there was also my sloppiness and sloth, and bad hygiene. The disorder was hindering me from running a successful charter boat operation.

For years, I've regaled psychiatrists with graphic descriptions of my chronic sloppiness and sloth (like dashing out a cigarette in a half-full bottle of my girlfriend's 50 dollar moisturizer) and they suggested I take drugs—powerful, controlled substances. While there were some nonnarcotic drugs, they were generally ineffective. All of the side effects, but none of the productivity Amphetamine (i.e. speed), now that's the real monkey juice. Adderall, Dexedrine, Ritalin—these brand-name formulas release dopamine into my system, slowing me down and, paradoxically, making me more focused. Those pills have helped boost and regulate my executive functions, and I have become more organized, functioning, and normal. And while there may be a little high or buzz as a side effect (depending on the brand and dosage), the doctors didn't mention it would be followed by a bone-crushing low, and inconsolable sadness. They made a convincing case that I would function better, and because I had ADHD, I'd say "okay" and play along.

The Coast Guard, however, would not play along. They don't allow the use of amphetamines by a charter boat captain, which includes any controlled substance prescribed by a doctor. The Coast Guard will randomly test for amphetamines, pot, cocaine, and opioids, and they don't care about the note from your quack professing that you have ADHD. (It's a controversial condition that is not even in the DSM-5, but caffeine intoxication is.) Nor will they care if you have a legit script. (PS: Too much caffeine can cause ADHD symptoms, too.)

If you fail the drug test, bye-bye captain's license.

But I had heard of a new, nonnarcotic ADHD medication. I forget the name, but it was not a controlled substance, and from what the good Dr. Bombay said, (by the way, I loved Dr. Bombay—and I think it was a shame when I learned that the state took away his right to practice in Manhattan. I thought he was a visionary...far far ahead of his time in neuro pharmacology) it seemed to be working wonderfully for people, so I tried it. After a week, it seemed to calm me down. I was focused, less impulsive, and more interested in details (although it did aggravate my already shrieking tinnitus). Once when I was methodically washing the saltwater off my reels, I remember thinking, "Wow, this is cool. This must be what normal people feel like!" I cleaned longer and more efficiently. I cared. I was getting things done. I respected order and structure. I was in the moment. But then, as it always does, something started twitching, or burning, or I had lock jaw and was unable to talk on the phone at all, or the dog would not go near me. All you want to do is read manuals or do grout work in your bathroom on these drugs, and god forbid someone interrupts you, they will instantly sense your disdain for them (note: you can not be in a relationship on ADD medication), or something else happens that eventually made me flush them down the toilet.

I had given up on ADD medication for years, then, one day, my internist told me about a new drug that hit the market called Vyvanse. I thought, "It does have a nice benign ring to it." It did not sound sinister like Crystal Meth (which it is) but Vyvanse sounded like a feminine hygiene product: "Are you a little musky down there? Try Vyvanse!" Or it sounded to me like a brand name for a pineapple soda. Anyway, Vyvanse is literally crystal meth. Look up the bonds and molecular structure, etc. To argue that they are, in any way, different is semantics.

So I tried Vyvanse. I took a white and green, 30-milligram capsule, and within just 20 minutes, I felt the need to empty my pockets of the normal debris of old useless receipts and Snickers bar wrappers. Then, I started organizing my wallet. Next, I was drawn out to my car, were I started throwing stuff out and organizing the trunk and glove compartment. I drove to the car wash and vacuumed out my car. After that, I drove down to the boatyard. Instantly, I felt a warm sensation while I cleaned my boat. Something I've never felt. I mean, I do occasionally clean, but it's always haphazard, like a fire drill, last-minute before customers arrived. Hence, a lot of stuff was overlooked (for example, I'd often leave a dump in the toilet un-flushed—this should never happen). I'd never got a feeling of satisfaction out of it. I never understood people who said they loved cleaning because it calmed them down, but now, on Vyvanse, I understood what they meant. I no longer felt the need to go stab a Mako shark in the head with a harpoon. I wanted to clean! I first flushed out my salt-corroded motor with fresh water for the first time. Someone once showed me how to do it, but I had problems hooking up the hose. Now, I was really into it. I mean, *really* into it. I even cleaned the head!

The point is: I was not in my normal state of seeking an adrenaline high, rushing to go fish; or going to a massage parlor for a rub and tug in Riverhead. No, I was in the moment. I had a new appreciation for my belongings. My tackle, my old rods—I cherished them. I wanted to protect them. I got out the WD-40 and thoroughly cleaned each reel and rod with added attention. I'd finish one task, and then move right on to the next. I finally felt like a normal, focused person. I remember thinking, "This new drug, Vyvanse, could be a real game changer!"

I sat down and composed an email, with no typos! I wrote to my mother, father, and sister, and I told them that I had finally found the right medication for my chemical imbalance and that this Vyvanse drug could, indeed, be a real game changer! Please note: when someone professes excitedly to you that they have been prescribed an ADD stimulant that they just went on last week and it's a real "game changer," turn and run from this person, because there's going to be hell to follow. Sure they will do well for a couple weeks, but then a monumental, bone-crushing, physical and emotional crash followed by an inconsolable emptiness that even the presence of a golden retriever puppy can't fix will come. Maybe I was just too sensitive, but it was awful. Because I'm lazy and have dyslexia, I can take liquid crack and, worse, crystal meth. Don't do it unless you are ready to ride out the possible crash when you come down. You will feel utter hopelessness, and you will never be the same. Life is hard and brutal enough if you're trying to make a living or support yourself and a family. There really is no "game changer," there is only controlling your diet, exercising, and hard work.

Nevertheless, I was enjoying the subtle, non-euphoric industry that the ADHD drug provided. In fact, I was considering calling my mother—a sweet, hardworking lady, if a bit of an enabler—and professing to her that I had once again found the drug and it was a "game changer." But then, I remembered, years earlier, when I went on Ritalin, I emailed just about everyone I knew, that I had a chemical imbalance and this drug, Ritalin, would correct it. Everything would be different.

Three days later, I was crushing the pills up and snorting them; the stuff was delicious and addicting as hell. Sure, it helped me focus, primarily on getting my hands on some more Ritalin. The goddamn stuff is marvelous and, by the way, also comes in a delightful green and white time release capsule for the holidays! One time, completely disgusted with myself, I dumped the bottle into a dumpster. The next day, I climbed into the dumpster to retrieve the tasty little nuggets. In reality, they're not as good as Adderall or Dexedrine, and they only work for about an hour, then leave you in a useless, depressed state. God, is the amphetamine-low bad.

Anyway, I was enjoying the industry this lovely drug provided. I was into cleaning, not running around with my head cut off, but dowsing everything with liberal amounts of Soft Scrub and some horrendous toxin called On & Off, which is primarily used to remove barnacles from ship bottoms. I inhaled so much of this stuff over the years, I'm surprised I have not grown a third ball. Sure, it removed pesky stains, but it also killed nasal hair and brain cells.

Now, on the "monkey juice," I was really cleaning—deliberately, methodically—and I was using executive function. I was not picking up the phone every two minutes and babbling to my retarded friends. What a waste of time that seemed. Finally, I was displaying composure and resolve. The problem: All you want to do is clean, and you don't want to talk to anyone, at all!

Things were great on Vyvanse until somehow, some way, my left nut shot up into my stomach and lodged itself there. It was early in the morning; I was at the marina getting my boat ready for my a.m. trip. There's no other way to say it: my ball, my testicle, was in my stomach. It wasn't necessarily painful, like shrieking pain, but it was unpleasant, for sure. It was not right.

Though I'd never had one before, I suppose it felt like a hernia. I was afraid to move. I was not in pain, but there was an unusual feeling. Not as bad as getting your zipper stuck on the head of your cock—that's brutal! (see *There's Something About Mary*) In fact, there is no real *painful* pain. It just felt not, well, not right. Odd, it felt…. Well, it felt just like a ball had gone into my stomach. Now, all that wonderful euphoric focus I had for cleaning the boat was directed at how I was going to dislodge my left ball from my stomach.

At that very moment, with my ball embedded somewhere in my lower groin, I saw five eager Groupon customers with coolers and rods in hand heading down the dock toward my boat. The a.m. trip! It was probably 5:30 a.m. What should I do? Cancel the trip? Call an ambulance? Go to the hospital? Should I tell these people I have a ball in my stomach? Had anyone else had this?

I told the eager and excited customers that I would be right with them to help them with their cooler. Then, I shut the door of my 28-foot Bertram and hid inside the cabin. Though warmhearted, I am a nervous, often weird and creepy person at times. And all these ADHD medications I'd been on (and I have tried them all) have side effects. One is that they make you incredibly antisocial. All you want to do is clean and fix stuff or play video games like a crystal meth addict.

In general, ADHD medications are not good for social activities. The charter boat business is entertainment. I needed to talk to the people: regale them with funny stories, ask them about their kids, etc. I had to remember their names—customers love their names. On ADHD medication, however, all I wanted to do was stay in the cabin and organize my sinker bucket. In my mind, talking to someone was a complete waste of fucking time. Why am I talking to you when I could be putting name tags on my socks?

I'm not articulate to begin with, but on the drug, I immediately had slurred speech. My jaw got tight, my eyes had that beady, full-out crackhead look. Any cop would've arrested me for suspicion of being under the influence. Oh, and I was never funny on my ADHD meds. I don't think anyone can be. Adderall is not a funny drug. I'm not sure I remember ever being all that funny on cocaine either. I remember being barricaded in rooms with other people; we thought we were cool. But I don't remember laughing, in fact I remember the laughter stopping as soon as the yayo came out, and I am a funny motherfucker. Funny is all I got. The stuff throws off your timing. It make one linear, while comedy is spontaneous, fractured, improvised. You don't want to improve on coke; you can't. I used to be a comic, a good one! Though I had tough mental glitches that caused me to shut down and become pensive—never good to be self-conscious as a comic. Entitlement issues (I stole some jokes) also really hurt me in that industry.

I often had everyone laughing on the boat. Certainly, Jimmy George didn't hire me on the *Nicole Marie* for my cleaning ability; he hired me because I was a funny mother fucker, and good with customers. On Adderall, however, customers scared the shit out of me. They made me twitch; I was sure, and I'm still pretty certain, that the twitching came from some heinous neurological condition that runs in my family and had remained dormant until this time (I believe I have a nice blend of MS, Parkinson, and ALS).

So, like I said, all I wanted to do was work on the tackle, or clean, or perhaps do some gentle flossing. But take a group of people fishing? Hell no! I didn't even want to pick up the phone. I felt like I was on acid.

Inside the cabin, I Googled: ADHD meds, testicle shrinkage/receding. Some PDF came up from the New England School of Medicine, but there was no quick answer. It's always like this when you go to the web for reassurance; you're hoping for, "Oh, it's nothing." But 90 percent of the time, Googling health stuff is far from reassuring. It is always terrible, especially that awful website, WebMD; no one gets reassured on that thing. You seek comfort and want to hear that it's probably nothing, but instead, they basically tell you that you would be better off dead.

The customers were there, they had driven from far away, and they had a prepaid Groupon voucher. I had no other options but to take them. All I could do was go on the trip and hope the renegade ball would dislodge itself. I have sensitive balls to begin with; I hate having them sucked on! I wanted the ball out. But I didn't want it to just pop out like a ping-pong ball or shoot out as if from a high-powered splat ball weapon, nor did I want it to come out slowly, like delivering a newborn baby. I wanted it to come out softly, as edamame slides out of it shell at a sushi restaurant—gentle and smooth.

I was going through the motions of running the trip, but the customers must have picked up on my mood. I was obviously pensive. You would be too if your left nut had gone missing. Sure, I was focused, like the ad for Vyvanse said I would be, but now I was primarily focused on whether or not my ball would drop. By the way, what the ad for Vyvanse fails to say is that your ability to multitask would be completely thrown out the window.

Thankfully, about an hour into the trip, it eventually dislodged. The ball dropped. Hallelujah! That's a great feeling when it passes, like a hemorrhoid I once had when I was living in Manhattan. Indulge me for a second, this thing was a motherfucker. It developed over a few days, until I could no longer walk. All I did was sit in bed on my hands and knees, spreading my ass cheeks out and rocking. Something had to be done, the pain was brutal. Bent over, I limped five blocks to a 24-hour CVS; got some Preparation H; put it on the golf ball-size, shrieking, unwelcome appendage; and *bang*! Within seconds, it seemed, no more hemorrhoid! Total emancipation from discomfort! I don't think I've ever been happier. What a great product! Buy stock! Like Viagra, it always works. At one point, I had a screaming anus, the next, no pain at all. I don't know who I would be more impressed with at a party: Steve Jobs, or the guy who invented Preparation H. I might literally hug that motherfucker!

Chapter 20

Caotian Cruntch: My Wakeup Call

In my defense, I was never that crazy or reckless. I fished largely nights, 12 miles from Montauk. It's not as congested as the Long Island Sound, where many people have been killed in boating accidents. For instance, in 1981, a recreational boat called the *Karen E* got caught between a tugboat and the barge it was pulling. Everyone on the boat died, including two children, their mother, and a family friend. The father was the sole survivor and told his side of story: The 41-foot sport fisherman ran behind a tugboat towing a barge 1000 yards behind and became caught on a towing cable (perhaps, and this is just a guess, the driver of the sportfisherman did not understand that the three white lights and a green one meant towing underway) and got pulled up like a zip line between two trees and crashed into the huge un-lit barge, which was carrying cement to Boston.

Another boating disaster took place in 1951 on a vessel out of Montauk: a 42-foot party boat named the FV *Pelican*. The boat was down a motor and overloaded with passengers (the maximum capacity rules have changed because of this tragedy); a sudden storm hit, and two successive waves capsized the boat. Over 45 passengers, including the boat's captain, Eddie Carroll, drowned. Some of the survivors were saved by other boats.

*

I knew what the lights meant when a barge was towing. I could tell what a submarine looked like, too. We probably saw one on roughly two out of 10 trips; their wakes were enormous. There were often boat races in Bock Channel. Sailboats are not well lit; many only have a red mast light that can easily blend in with the smoke stack lights of distant New London, Connecticut. You can think a boat is miles away, and all of a sudden, there's a 50-foot slope 100 feet off your bow. So, you can bet your ass I was on guard and constantly checking my radar.

I was pretty anal. I wouldn't let anyone drink or smoke pot on my boat, and if I sensed they were on pills (which is easy to detect since pill poppers become very chatty), I would turn around and drop them off at the dock. Whenever I had to do this, I'd tell them to come back when they were sober. I preached at everyone. When my drinking friends asked if they could bring beers on my boat, I'd tell them they could only bring one and they couldn't drink it until we were on the way home. After they caught a big fish, I would say, "Look at this, look how gorgeous the moon is, look how good the fishing is! Do you really need to drink?" I was brutal, oftentimes a real dick, but for good reason: booze and competitive, productive fishing simply don't mix.

Think about it: this doesn't happen in other sports, does it? Should a partner show up to play tennis after he's had a few? Or what about recreational basketball? No drinkers there. But for some reason, people on boats need to party. Well, not on my boat.

Yes, it was about safety. We used 12-ounce sinkers and sharp hooks, and things become dangerous when some drunk guy starts swinging around in the dark. Two beers on the water is the equivalent of six on land. Any charter boat captain will tell you that the guy that feels the need to crack open a beer on the way to the fishing grounds won't be as productive as the fishermen who are not drinking. Drinking and fishing make a bad pair; if you think they don't, you're the guy that people wish hadn't come on trip.

I have never had a great night of fishing with a drunk customer. People lose their balance a little, but, worse, they lose their ambition. Two beers is all it takes to drain someone's ambition—like watching Jennifer Aniston's face drop when Brad broke the news that he was leaving her, or when Louis C.K. read the article in the *Times* that his career was essentially over—to the point that he doesn't really care if he catches a fish. I brought out a bunch of drunk cops once, and it was horrible. I like cops, even though I've never gotten one of those fuckers to give me a PBA card! I have a few close friends who are cops, but they won't give me the card because they don't want to be associated with me when I end up in a child pornography ring; fair enough . . . whatever. Cops see bad shit all the time. They are the first people called when there's a suicide or when an 18-year-old kid gets thrown through the windshield doing 70 because she was texting. Anyway, I wanted them to have a good time. Everyone was catching except the one guy who was drunk and who was kind of the ring leader. He lost three fish at the boat because he tightened the drag when I told him to loosen it. He became belligerent. We had to kick him off the boat later; I can spot oxycodone addiction instantly. My closest fishing buddy, cousin Kenny, died from it, but not before he put his mother and his entire neighborhood through hell for years.

My point is that I'd had a bad year, but I was generally pretty careful. I needed to catch fish.

*

My wakeup call came on a calm August summer day. I was headed out fishing and saw a bunch of boats clustered at a normal fishing spot (Endeavor Shoals) about three miles from Montauk Harbor. That spot often held fish, so I figured the bite

165

was on. I didn't pay it any attention and continued out to do some fluke fishing.

Later that day, I found out that it was not a bite at all. A sinking boat and a mayday call had drawn the crowd. In a matter of minutes, a boat had made the mayday call, and then dramatically, with its bow in the air, it had sunk—in front of many eyewitnesses. It wasn't just a recreational boat, either, but a registered charter boat (though I had never heard of the boat before; it was not an established boat of the main fleet, but a renegade operation like mine).

The boat was an old 1970s Hatteras named *Crunch Time* with a gas (not diesel) engine, which is scary. Gas explodes, diesel does not. Apparently, this guy, like me, was having water intrusion problems all along. On the day it sank, something must have cracked and started letting water in. There are so many ways for water to get into the engine blocks. But something happened, and hundreds of gallons of water flooded into the entire engine room and cabin. Quickly. The boat started sinking.

I was surprised that this had happened. I've been in similar situations and found that a handful of terrified customers armed with five gallon buckets (using the assembly line method with two guys in the engine room handing the bucket to a guy on deck who dumps the water overboard, then hands the bucket back for another pail) and motivated by the genuine terror at the very real threat of drowning can usually put a decent dent in the most spectacular water intrusion volume, at least keeping the water below the top of the engine head.

Unfortunately, this was not what happened aboard *Captain Crunch*. The water went over the engines, and the boat stalled. It went down quickly, bow up, with five bewildered customers diving for their lives and swimming to other boats for rescue. Since they all survived, of course, there's a comic element to it. Until someone gets hurt, it's all funny.

Luckily, it was in the middle of summer, and there were a bunch of charter and private boats to retrieve the passengers, each of whom knew how to swim. So, all six people were unharmed. For days, people were finding debris from the boat: a cooler here, an engine room door there, a radar cap somewhere nearby.

Now, it's sad that Captain Crunch went down. It's always sad when a boat goes down. But it was not a tragedy. No one got hurt. The "what ifs" kept haunting me. I kept thinking: What if it had been foggy out that day? It very well could have been; fog is common in Montauk. The Coast Guard can't find a body in the fog, nor can a sea plane or helicopter. What if the tide had been going out? Those people would've been pushed out to sea or maybe hit by another boat. What if it was raining and no other boats had been around to rescue the passengers? What if his VHF radio was down? What if it was May and the water was 50 degrees? Or December off of Cox Ledge? All those people would have perished.

The story resonated with me.

That night, it hit me like a freight train. The *Crunch* could have easily been me: I could not continue to be a charter boat captain in Montauk. I simply did not have what it took.

Quite frankly, I never even deserved a boat. I should be floating around in an inflatable tube in a pool in a structured living environment. And after that wakeup call, I'd had enough. If I didn't stop now, someone could get hurt. Perhaps I could captain a small guide boat, but I didn't have the mechanical skill, interest, or aptitude to maintain a big, safe, functional inboard charter boat. Hats off to the guys who can do this. It's all about acceptance. Look, I wish I was a lion, but I'm a lamb, and that's not bad thing. I just don't have what it takes. Cognitively, I'm lazy. Mechanical know-how I lack. Every charter boat captain in Montauk knows how to change belts on water pumps, or their mates do. This is basic stuff, but I did not know how to do it. Yes, I could've learned how to do it, but the desire was never there. I just wanted the adrenaline and the glory of landing big fish.

The day after the *Crunch Time* sank, I had a close call with some customers (all over 400 pounds) from Groupon. I was night fishing and i got a call to see if I was available the next day, they had a voucher, I was too busy to check my phone for weather, or apparently the VHS radio, and made the mistake of asking one of the customers what the weather was going to be like, the guy fished a lot and had his own boat so I figured he knew I meant marine weather, anyway he professed that it was going to be a " beautiful day", so i booked the trip for the morning. The next day it was blowing 20 knots from the northeast. My new bilge pumps were not working, and water was pouring into my boat through the scuppers and into the bilge through cracks in the old unsealed hatches on the Bertram. There was nothing I could do. I looked into the engine room and there was 10 inches of water creeping up the engine block. My passengers were in no shape to bail, so I headed for shore limping along with one engine at 5knots. A mile off the point I noticed that the boat was listing heavily to port and barely making way under the hard outgoing tide. So I told the guys we were not going to make it around the point, and that I was going to beach the boat, on the other side of the lighthouse, at a place called Turtle Cove; We were about ten 20 minutes away and I was not sure we would make it, so I called the Coast Guard and announced my plans. As the wind was now from the north, it was remarkably calm in turtle cove, so in about 4 foot of water, one by one, the fat fucks got on to the swim Platform and reluctantly entered the water. The coast Guard, showed up about ten Minutes later and jumped on with a pump and bailed me out. Then escorted me back to port; I must say, in all my rescues THe Coast Guard, were alway respectful and efficient; they were great. Right after that, I put my boat up for sale. I listed it for

$1,000, citing that it only had one engine. I eventually sold on Craigslist for $1000.

Chapter 21

Rescues at Sea

I could not find a buyer for my boat, and the calls kept coming in; people wanted to fish. So, against my better judgement, I continued chartering customers with only one engine on the Bertram. As a result, the Coast Guard rescues became far more frequent.

I will say that all my rescues where legitimate: I never called the Coast Guard out of convenience just to get a free tow home. My calls were never trivial. In every case, there was real danger of drowning. I've been rescued a total of seven times in 15 years, five of which took place in my final year as a charter boat captain. I often had the towing service come and get me, and once, when my engine broke down, I drifted around all night until the guy from BoatUS (a boating insurance company) woke up at 8 a.m. and came out and got me three hours later.

Every issue came up after I had pulled anchor or was anchored and taking waves over the back. Every time, there was water intrusion or rough seas. I must say that every time the Coast Guard came, they were excellent. A respectful and professional lot. They never reproached me, and it was obvious that they'd drilled a lot because their boat handling and boarding skills were first-rate. Even the last time—when they wrote me as many citations as the guy on the Exxon *Valdez*—they were always decent and professional. The most citations I got at once was after one particularly hair-raising trip.

It was a Groupon trip, and as I mentioned before, most groups were surprisingly pleasant: they either used to fish in Montauk and were coming back to try it again after many years, or they were flat-out newbies. They often had a happy but dazed look, like they were about to go on a ride on an amusement park. Boy, did they not know the half of it! Little did they know that their Groupon trip would consist of drifting around on a smelly, dangerous boat with an eccentric retard for five hours.

Before Groupon, I got all losers. And I mean losers, without exception. Complete and total losers. I lot of diehard trophy striped bass fisherman are losers—grown men in their 50s and 60s who failed at most things in life and now needed to kill and show off their trophies on Facebook. I was one of them. I, too, needed to catch a big bass. Most of them would hide their mental illness, but it always surfaces, in one form or another, during the course of the trip, and I would have that *aha!* moment. No wonder the guy called me. Especially if he answered my ad on Craigslist. It was never two or three guys; it was always a loner. Many of my customers were living with their mothers, and all seemed to have pending lawsuits—usually a workers' compensation suit.

Think about it: Who but the destitute would book a trip with *Second Choice Charters*?

*

When I first started with Groupon, the trips went pretty well, if I do say so myself. There were, however, several setbacks and obstacles.

With only one working engine on my 28-foot Bertram (it had no name on its stern, other than the barely visible *Joey V*, but being a trademark notorious deep-V Bertram, I should've named it the "Pukefest").

One rescue was when I had a single passenger, a guy who had read my book, *Caught*, and had always wanted to fish with me. As we were steaming back from a successful diamond jigging trip, we were both up on the bridge, and the good engine started to overheat. I climbed down and opened the hatch. There was steam everywhere. I saw right away that a belt had broken on the water pump that cooled the ending. I had the tools and the extra built to fix it, so I got to work.

It was a big, outgoing tide, and we were in a middle of a fierce rip. I wasn't sure if I should throw the anchor or not. I did, and it landed us right before a huge rip called the Elbow. So now, we were anchored, but the boat had tremendous death rocks, pitching violently from one side to another. The bigger problem was that I couldn't get the frightened passenger down from the bridge. The poor guy was holding on for his life; he could have touched the water, that's how far the boat would veer to each side.

I couldn't work on the engine in these conditions. So, I went up and cut the anchor. But this did not help much; we were now helplessly drifting into a dangerous rip with six-foot curling waves. I said myself, "If we take one over the back, I'm calling the Coast Guard." We did, of course, and about 100 gallons entered the cockpit. I made the call. It was not a mayday, but I told them my predicament. By the time they arrived (only half an hour later—a quick response), we had passed through the rip into rough but safe water, and the bilge had emptied most the water.

They did not give me a hard time and towed us in. The customer insisted on paying me.

*

My slip at my new marina, Diamond Cove, was a challenge to get out of with one engine. When there was the proponent south west wind it was easy enough, as the one engine wanted to push toward the starboard side, the South west wind would correct it and I could inch out. It took me a while, and all the bumping and pushing off other parked boats frustrated and embarrassed my customers. If there was a north wind, rare in the summer time, I was totally screwed because the engine and wind pushed the boat in the same direction; right into the charter fleet at neighboring Westlake marina. That's why I began to drop off and pick up customers at more accessible marinas. A couple of times, I was forced to start the bad port engine, which would instantly blow a huge black plume of smoke into the neighboring marina (West Lake), sending people over yelling. This type of inauspicious send-off made us all look like idiots, and it would often lead, as well it should, to early and unwanted suspicion among the Groupon customers, who would question my abilities as a competent skipper.

No sense in all of us looking like fools. I would instruct the customers to meet at the gas dock at Star Island—the nicest marina around, and they had a very accessible floating gas dock platform, which was easy to push off from. So, while I was playing bumper pool with other boats, the customers waited at this other marina.

On one particular day, there was a slight north wind, and I only had one working engine (the port engine). So, with the north wind pushing my bow and the port engine pushing in the same direction, I couldn't make the turn and get out of my narrow slip. The only way I could turn the boat was by backing into a bulkhead or pylon and throwing the boat in reverse. I felt like I was onto something. I must've really looked like I knew what I was doing to the onlookers that had gathered; the boat pipetted well off the pylon and got us out of a jam. I bet good old Joshua Slocum did not have this move. However, I came too close to the starboard side trim tab and ripped it off. This wasn't the end of the world, I thought, but little did I know at the time, the trim tabs were built into the transom of the boat that went into the bilge. Now, before the customers got on the boat, I had water pushing into these four small holes.

When I finally got Star Island Marina, the designated drop-off/pickup spot, I saw the happy Groupon group descending the dock, blissfully unaware that the boat was taking on water. Just watching them walk down the dock, I could tell it was going to be an easy, fun trip. For one, they appeared not to be loaded, fat drunks, which was always good—just one father, his friend, and two boys probably 16 to 17 years old. The friend looked to be about 50 years old and in lean, good shape; he was from Lancaster, Pennsylvania, and had not been in the ocean in years. And before that, never.

As I mentioned earlier, I've always preferred it when no one had experience. The guys that know a little are usually the troublemakers. The father, upon first impression, seemed like he might fit into the troublemakers category, but I couldn't tell yet.

It was a nice day. I was in high spirits when I loaded the guys onto the Bertram. It was clean—clean for me, anyway—and there were no complaints. One guy did remark that the boat looked like the one from *Jaws*, but I let it slide.

I had stopped telling Groupon customers that I was only running on one engine. It didn't serve much purpose, and most didn't seem to mind going under 18 knots. We cruised at a gentlemanly speed of eight knots: What's the rush? Even when I did tell them about the one working engine, they rarely complained.

Conditions were perfect. It was an outgoing tide pulling us in the right direction with little wind, so we were moving at a brisk eight knots. It was a full-day, seven-hour trip—no problem at six knots. In an hour and a half, we'd be getting to the fishing ground. I wanted to break up the trip a bit by bending the rods at the point with some live porgies (a bait fish), but the waves on the outgoing rips were too large for the Bertram, and I didn't want to take the chances of getting anyone sick.

So, I pushed on past the point to a place called Frisbee's, five miles from the point or another half hour at our generous eight-knot clip. I warned them early that fluke and seabass fishing had not been good, but we might get lucky. Either way, we would target them for an hour and wait for the tide to change at the point. Sure enough, as expected, the bottom fishing was pretty lame— no keeper fluke; maybe five sea bass, one may have been keeper; some skates and dog fish. Still, we were having fun.

I was happy for these guys. The bass fishing on live porgies had been red hot. It was 2 p.m. on a Tuesday. The tide was good. There would not be many boats around, and if there were, it was only because I shot my mouth off. (That's always been my problem. I've told too many people about sacred fishing holes just because I wanted them to like me, I suppose. I was such a blabbermouth. It got me in trouble a few times when someone told me something intended only for me. That's what happens in fishing: You show your friends a spot and how to fish it, and the next year, they act like they discovered it themselves and treat you like an idiot. I've learned to have second thoughts about telling people my fishing secrets.)

I digress. "Guys, the tide is starting to slacken," I told them. "Let's grab some porgies and hook some big bass." They were all excited, having picked up on my genuine enthusiasm. We were going the crush the bass, I had no doubt. The wind was right (light southwest on the floodtide), the tide perfect, and the bass were there—big stripers, 40 pounders. I was really excited to see these guys land a few. And they were also into releasing them, which was a bonus.

After a while, I told one the guys to take the wheel, aim right for the lighthouse, and not to hit anything a like lobster pot or another boat. "If you see one, call me," I said and went down to tie the rigs.

A half hour later, we hit a place called the Slot, about three miles from the lighthouse. I did recall the boat feeling a little sluggish and heavy in the water, but I'd been too busy readying the boats and changing out the rods from fluke to bass to pay it much attention. I jumped down from the Bertram's bridge and went into cabin to get the porgy rods. When I opened cabin doors to retrieve the rods, I saw the water pushing up the hatches in the cabin. I had a sinking feeling (pardon the pun). It was not the usual embarrassing situation like the popular commercials ("Do you want to get away?"). It was not awkward; it was scary. I was terrified. I've only had two or three white-knuckle experiences, like: "Oh my god, we're going to die for sure!" But it was a nice clear day. The water was 70 degrees. We all had cell phones, and I had a working GPS, VHF radio, and plenty of life preservers. While shocked and alarmed, I thought that we would make it.

I opened the engine hatch—at this point an academic exercise because I knew, judging by the water in the cabin and the way the boat was listing, what I would find. Namely: massive water intrusion. In this case, there had to be a good 300 gallons already in the engine room, and more was coming in quick. I did not know where it all came from. There were no cracked hoses I could duct tape, I could see no valve to close. It didn't matter. We were sinking, and sinking fast. The water was up to my waist (I'm roughly five-foot-ten), about three-quarters of the way up the side of the engine blocks. I looked up the hatch and yelled sternly and deadly serious to the Groupon customers: "This boat is sinking! This is a Mayday! Put life jackets on!"

At first, they thought I was joking. The kids smiled. "Look, I am not fucking joking!" Luckily, I had a couple of five-gallon buckets that I'd brought along to serve as a live well for the porgies; without them, we would've sunk within five minutes, for sure. There were no other boats around, but the tide was incoming, so even if we sank, some boat would eventually notice us swimming. All I was thinking about was that I could end up like the *Crunch Time*.

I grabbed the buckets and handed them to the father, who, I could tell, went to the gym; he was a little heavy, but had big arms and probably weighed about 250 pounds. The other guy was lean, but fit. "Listen," I said, "you guys start bailing assembly-line style. I'm going to point the boat towards the lighthouse. Bail like your life depends on it: if water gets over the engines, this boat will sink." They went to work; I must say, they were great. They were probably averaging 100 buckets an hour, which is pretty good.

The other kid was with me up on the bridge. He was loving it the whole way. My VHF was on the blink, so my maydays were not being returned. I told the kid to use his cell phone to call 911. He did, and we got transferred not to the Coast Guard, which would've been more helpful, but to the East Hampton Police Department. The officer who took our call served as a middleman, if you will. I told them we were in a dire predicament, that we were five souls sinking three miles from the point, and we were headed to the lighthouse, but we probably wouldn't make it before the boat sank. We needed a PAN-PAN (a distress alert to boats in the area to be on lookout) and a mayday released. I was terrified.

We hung up the phone. The cop called back and said he relayed the information to the Coast Guard. But an hour passed, and they just were not coming. Why didn't I call the sea tow? I had the insurance. The guys kept bailing.

I knew how to handle this. I called back and told the cop, "Listen, this is the last time you'll hear from us. This is not a joke." I read off coordinates from the GPS. "We're headed north to Montauk Point Lighthouse. I will beach the boat off the concession stand. (As great as the Coast Guard is at rescuing people and boats, they don't know the local lingo for big landmarks, like "The Elbow" or "Turtle Cove." Most of them are from the Midwest, which is why they need GPS coordinates. That's why all boats should be required to have GPS and EPIRB devices on them.)

As I turned the boat, I felt it list and sway. I got under three knots. I looked down, and the guys were still working like pros: slow, stable, and efficient. They shoveled bucket after bucket. Still, the water lurked dangerously close to the tops of the engines. We had probably taken on over 700 gallons. When, and if, the water hit the injectors, wires, and starter, the boat would stall out.

As we sputtered along, I wondered if my charter boat insurance had been canceled. If so, I wondered if it was too late to get charter boat insurance. I pathetically asked the kid to Google "GEICO" to see if I could start a new policy.

The kids, by the way, were loving it. "Are you really going to beach it?" they kept asking. They couldn't wait. While the friend was holding up okay bailing, the father looked red faced and worn out. He could've easily stroked out. I had the kid drive the boat, and I went to relieve the father. I bailed 10 buckets and handed them to the other kid to dump overboard. The water was receding slowly, now covering half the engine blocks.

Finally, a solid hour had gone by, and still no Coast Guard. We arrived at the point. The water had dropped significantly, only a quarter up the engine block, so I didn't feel the need to beach her yet. What was the point? I started to work my way north at three knots toward the harbor. We were 30 feet from shore in three feet of water.

The father bellowed: "I thought you were going to beach it!"

I told him calmly that I could, and would, but we would not get much closer anyway, and disembarking the vessel could be dangerous. "Let's wait 10 more minutes. To see if the Coast Guard shows up. They'll come with pumps and escort us back the remaining way; it's much safer. If they don't show up, I'll beach it."

Then, right by Shagwong, we saw the Coast Guard cutter heading east. Did they see us waving? I brought flares out and set one off. When that didn't work, I called the East Hampton police again and told them that the Coast Guard was passing us and that they should look west toward the shore. Finally, they saw us and turned towards us. Relief replaced dread. "Here they come!" we shouted. They boarded us with hoses and pumps, tied us off, and started to pull us back to Montauk Harbor.

To lighten the mood, I told the father, "Look at the bright side, you got a free trip!"

He was not amused.

It was clear he was trying to process what had happened to him. He saw the Coast Guard poking around the boat, looking for this and that, and asking me all kinds of questions about the boat and my captain's license, all of which implied that I was a gypsy charter service on a boat that was unfit for the sea. "Where is your license? Do you have one? And your registration?" The boat was such a mess, I struggled to find these things.

When the father saw that I was vulnerable, he struck, right in front of the Coast Guard (mostly young, embarrassed men).

"Hey, you almost killed us, I need to be compensated," the father said.

I had been doing well over the past few days and had $5,000 in my pocket. I did feel bad, so I said I'd give him $500 bucks. He said okay, and we shook on it. I went into the cabin to count out the cash. I had the money, but the more I thought about it, $500 did not seem right. Shit happens! When a cab breaks down, does the cab driver give you money? Hell no. He tells you to get out hail another cab. I peeled off $325 and told the concerned opportunist I would PayPal him the rest that night; a boldface lie. The guy did not pursue the remainder of the balance.

I thought about how he might sue. Imagine that court case. The judge would ask: what was the name of the boat. Second choice charters...I mean if booking a boat with your family are you sure you want to go on something called Second choice... Judge: how did you hear about second choice? Answer: Groupon...group discount ..... case dismissed.

Once in the harbor, the Star Island Marina wanted nothing to do with my 1974 Bertram. I was still escorted to Star Island Yacht Club, one of the nicest in the east coast (and the only place that didn't know me), and the last thing they wanted to see was my piece of shit boat. But too late. I rushed up on the slings to the lift, and they pulled the boat out. We instantly saw the problem. Water came pouring out of the stern from six holes, right where I had clipped the trim tab off that morning. I knew exactly what had happened. I had knocked of that trim tab with my "fancy maneuvering," thinking I was a genius who had made his old Uncle Slocum proud. Evidently, I was not so smart: the pylon had ripped the trim tab from the boat, and bolts connected the transom directly to the hull. The holes did not look big enough to bring in that much water, but they had.

Star Island charged me $700 for the emergency haul and 20 minutes of labor. I had to put $5,200 into the stern, where the holes were. I had the cash on me, so I told the mechanic to do it.

***

In the meantime, the tickets and summonses came from the Coast Guard:

- No registration
- Improper registration sticker on boat
- No number 4 for flotation device
- Unable to show proper captain credentials
- No charter sticker on boat
- Expired fire extinguisher
- Only one fire extinguisher
- Missing second fire extinguisher
- No waste disposable sticker on head

The good news was that I had flares and enough life preservers.

Chapter 22

Why I Write

Let's face it, times are tough. Funnier writers than me are have a hard time finding readers. I don't care what anyone says, reading is pretty much dead. No one reads anymore. People will argue with me, and publishers point to sales stats. And of course, high school and college kids are reading because they have to. Thank god for people over 75 years of age, who are not consumed with their phones and devices, and for the public library system down in Florida that recommends books for my mother, who bangs out a book a week and loves it! Unlike some of her peers, who simply watch Fox news and see Trump like this reality show (of which there will be a next season), my mother remains interested and engaged in life because of literature. Even alone, she knows she has a friend that, like a dog, is simply more tangible than the Internet and TV.

Of course there are still readers, just like there are cheese connoisseurs, rock climbers, chess players, snake charmers, and fire throwers. But readers appear to be becoming a subculture. On the whole, the general public does not read. And this is bad! A good book—not the shock-humor crap I bang out, but true literature like Jonathan Franzen's *Freedom*—is the best that the arts and humanities can offer, one with recurring themes and characters, a narrative arc, foreshadowing, plot, and great vocabulary.

People say they read, but when pushed, they admit they don't. "I'm far too busy," they say as they run home to binge watch Netflix and jam Häagen-Dazs down their gullets. I know some motherfuckers who can watch a whole show season in one night. They have all the time in the world—for that and browsing Tinder.

For Christmas 2019, I was given a book: *A Man for All Oceans* by Stan Grayson. The book was about a direct uncle of mine, Captain Joshua Slocum, who happened to do a family lineage chart. (Not the BS stuff on Ancestry.com, which has convinced millions of dumbass Americans that they had family members that were on the Mayflower! Have you seen the Mayflower? The fucking boat was only 50 feet long. It may have carried 50 people, tops.)

Anyway, Joshua Slocum was a world class boat builder, fisherman, captain, and sailor of commercial tall ships. And he was a writer! Learning this inspired me to write again.

Slocum was driven, hardworking, a gifted and accomplished boat builder, and a tough leader—in other words, he was nothing like me (granted, he didn't have to deal with constant Groupon calls and texts). He was also an expert celestial navigator; he sailed across the Atlantic many times and ran several commercial tall sailing ships with large crews across world carrying all sorts of cargo. He fought off mutiny (literally—physically) twice. When the tall ship industry got wiped out by the faster and more efficient steamship at the turn of the century, he moved back to Nova Scotia, where he was born overlooking the Bay of Fundy, and tried to be a farmer. But he did not take to that, so he built his own boat from scratch, the *Spray*, and sailed around the entire world.

I read the whole biography and realized that even though Slocum and I were related, the two of us had nothing in common. I felt less than. He was a driven disciplinarian, a task master, that captain of huge sailing ships. He also helped invent a new form of seine netting and brought it to Alaska (though his trip to the Cook Inlet ended with his boat getting wrecked). He was the first man to sail around the world—not just across the Atlantic but the entire globe—he was also the first to navigate the Straits of Magellan by himself. Many boats have been made to imitate and give tribute to the *Spray*.

Slocum was a badass in every way. The only similarity between the two of us came late in the book. Apparently, old Slocum had become a bit eccentric with age and some failures, as well as the loss of his beloved first wife, Virginia, who used to sail with him. And, as Slocum ran tall sailing ships, the invention of the steamship really took Slocum out, just like the car wiped out the horse and buggy driver. Slocum was seen as a bit of an anachronism. His famous boat, the *Spray*, had fallen into disrepair and was docked on Martha's Vineyard, and he spent all summer fiddling about with his boat. According to Stan Grayson, Slocum was prone to not buttoning up his trousers properly, and because sailors were not big on underpants in those days, his penis would often be hanging out his pants. He was even arrested after some children reported him, and he told the judge that he'd simply forgotten to button his pants; he went to jail 20 days as punishment for his "forgetfulness."

Chapter 23

Pump Out or When Duty Calls or Brown Gold

The timing was right when my friend called and asked me if I wanted to apply for a job running a town boat in Montauk. The town was looking for a licensed captain with experience in running a 23-foot center console outboard, he said, and he thought the job was right up my alley. Having recently failed as a Groupon charter captain, I simply didn't have the organizational or mechanical skills needed to run a full-time functioning charter boat service. So I was ready for a new job.

Sure, I needed the money, but this was bigger than that. Like I said earlier, I spent most of my adult life trying to insert myself into glamorous or cool careers I was underqualified for, and while I had periods of success and some nice paydays as a writer, these successes never blossomed into full careers. So, with the help of various twelve-step programs (I was on my knees a lot, praying) and a therapist, I started focusing on the importance of humility and becoming a worker among workers, and I finally accepted the fact that all jobs, no matter how menial, have dignity. My goal was simple: an honest day's work for an honest day's pay. Without asking my friend about the specifics of the boat job, I said sure. He gave me the number to call at the trustees' office.

I wondered what running the town boat would entail. Would I be checking mooring numbers and boat registrations? Making sure the estuaries and oyster fiends were protected and well-marked. Or perhaps supervising sailing regattas? Maybe it would be a launch boat, where I would shuttle trustees and board members to survey bulkheads that were in violation of zoning codes. I mean, how hard could it be?

As I was entertaining these pleasant images of my new career on the water, my good natured but gruff commercial fisherman friend called back. "By the way," he said, "when you call the trustees' office, the boat you're applying to run is called the *pump out* boat." Then, in a matter of fact way, he went on to describe the job requirements: "You'll be removing septic from large yachts, transporting it, and discarding it into a 100,000-gallon holding tank near the Coast Guard station. Hard work, but great tips."

He hung up. I sat there, despondent. Did he say septic? Reality was slowly sinking in. My friend was suggesting I apply for a job running a septic barge in Montauk Harbor.

*

Like most of us who live on "The East End," I was acquainted with the dire septic issues facing our Long Island waters. How could we not? Just about every other day, Channel 12 News runs a report on dangerous allergy blooms, high nitrogen levels, and toxic brown tides. I had heard about city beaches being closed due to septic/fecal runoff after storms. And wasn't it Havens Beach in Sag Harbor that was closed because of high nitrogen levels in the water?

The definition of "septic" is toxic and dangerous. In short, shit is nothing to play around with. In the one-day training class for the pump out boat job, we learned that, if handled without gloves, fecal exposure can lead to hepatitis, typhoid fever, cholera, norovirus, polio, *E. coli*, tapeworms, giardia, rotavirus, and so on. Years ago, I had the pleasure of hearing the Peconic Baykeeper, Kevin McAllister (an excellent public speaker), lecture eloquently about septic runoff issues, the importance of eelgrass, and the horrendous effects of lawn fertilizers and overbuilding shorelines with bulkheads.

So, I got it: Removing septic from Montauk Harbor (or any waterway) was an important and even an admirable job. I needed a job, and it was a good fit. But even though I desperately needed work, could I really envision myself pumping crap for 40 hours a week? When I got my captain's license and moved out to Montauk, my goal was to become a famous fisherman. I'd envisioned crowds of people waiting at the dock, straining their necks to get a peek at my customers' trophy catches as I confidently backed my boat into the slip.

I did not want to be the pump out guy! I certainly would not get invited to any parties—then again, I wasn't exactly lighting the Hamptons' party scene on fire to begin with. When I told my girlfriend about the gig, she was remarkably supportive. "Look," she said, "it's a great chance to work outdoors on the water." I rebutted, "I love the Grand Canyon, too, but I don't want to scrub Porta Potties in the visitor's parking lot for 40 hours a week."

I called my friend back to express my apprehensions and tell him I didn't think the job was for me. He patiently absorbed my concerns, and then he rattled off a list of my pump out boat predecessors. All of them were far more qualified than I was. Most were retired cops who were doing the job to stay busy, make a few extra bucks, and serve the community. One guy, "Sid," who had done the job for 17 years, was a retired, decorated Navy man (Sid has since moved away from Montauk, but I had the pleasure of meeting him before he did—a real gentlemen).

It's been said that Sid became an intrinsic part of the harbor, which makes sense to me.

The harbor operator at the time, who I would be training and working under, had the most impressive resume of all. He served in the Coast Guard for four years, had been running commercial fishing boats all over the world for decades, and later operated one of the nicest private yachts in Montauk. He was also a skilled diesel mechanic and boat builder. The point is this: If running the pump out boat was good enough for these guys, it sure as hell was good enough for this old burnout.

I also love the "campus" (if you will) of Montauk Harbor. Who wouldn't? I was primarily a night striped bass fisherman, so 100 nights a year, on the way back in from fishing, when all was calm just before daybreak, I'd pass beloved institutions: Gosman's ice house, Inlet Seafood, the public dock that housed all those great industrial draggers with seagulls perched on top of them, their heads buried in their chests in slumber. There were the crisp, orderly, white buildings of the Coast Guard station with their red shingled roofs and 40-foot cutters docked close by on floating docks, poised and eagerly awaiting the call to service.

Point is, I have never not been filled with gratitude every night that I enter into this wonderful harbor—this pearl cut into the outermost easterly tip of Long Island, jutting 120 miles into the Atlantic Ocean. So anything I could do to help this sacred place—one that has given me such immense pleasure over the years—which was now quickly (some feel sadly) changing from an idyllic fishing village and family beach town (the occasional crystal meth busts and domestic violence hiccups notwithstanding) to a high-end party destination, I would gladly do.

*

During the training classes, I found out there was a growing need for the pump out boat I'd be working on. The Harbor is getting fewer fishing boats and family cruisers and more huge, garish, plastic mega-yachts that one would expect to see anchored off the coast of Mykonos in the Greek Isles with the cast of *Jersey Shore* dancing off the bow while doing shots of Jägermeister.

Some marinas tried to add more public bathrooms to accommodate the influx of people, but they failed to meet the zoning requirements (or something like this), so people relied heavily on the heads (i.e. toilets) on the yachts. In short, there was a growing need for septic removal. Without a pump out boat, these yachts, which rarely left their slips, would (once full) certainly dump their waste in the harbor.

Let me quantify this with hard numbers. Last year, we pumped out an estimated 75,000 gallons of raw, untreated septic or, as I like to call it, Brown Gold.

*

Before I became a pump out operator, I thought it would be a sanitary operation. I mean, it was 2019, wasn't it?

Well, here's what I learned on day one of training: After tying the pump out boat to a yacht with a full septic tank, you pass a hose up to a crew member on the yacht with the correct fitting secured to the end of the hose. Once the yacht's septic tank is empty (usually about 20 minutes), the crew member returns the hose, and then you're off to the next boat. Once you've reached the pump out boat's 400-gallon capacity, it's time to unload all that crap at a secured holding tank near the Coast Guard station, where the sewage is kept in an airtight compartment, and there will be absolutely no leaking or spills.

Sounds simple and at least fairly clean, right? Well, yes— in theory, it is a clean operation. The hoses are vacuumed sealed.

We use gloves. We use hand sanitizer. We clean the boat and rinse off the hoses afterwards. We try not to spill a drop anywhere, neither in the water, nor on our boat, nor on the customer's boat.

But, as is the case on all boats, "shit happens." When you think of all the working parts, how could it not? The pump is working hard, pushing 12 to 15 gallons of septic a minute—that's a shitload of pressure. The hose chugs and moans and once in a while gets a sort of speed wobble/gyration where it starts to convulse, which is usually caused by paper towels, pantyhose, tampons, or some other debris that's been forced down the head.

Too much pressure on a four-inch hose and it'll eventually burst, sending a geyser of brown shit exploding out with enough power to knock someone off a horse. When this happens, septic waste spills all over the deck and we're up to the top of our work boots—and sometimes knee-deep—in raw fecal matter. After stopping the pump, we have to slowly drive our shit-caked pump out boat to the dock, tie up, and get busy cleaning.

There are also times when air clogs push 20 gallons of shit right back onto the deck. Clamps and cams give way with the sun and salt water, hoses dry out and crack, and you've got to clean up all the messes that these damages cause, too.

One time, while I was unloading my boat's haul at the Coast Guard station, their main holding tank overflowed, and the alarm didn't go off. I heard something splashing and looked up, only to see gallons of brown shit erupting and pouring out of an overflow valve like lava from a volcano. I ran back to turn off my pump, but, by that time, there was a 200-gallon puddle in the middle of the nearby parking lot. I called my supervisor; marine patrol stopped by; I applied a soap concentrate, got a wet vac, and started the cleanup that went well past sun down. By the next day, that parking lot was spotless.

*

The entire time driving the pump out boat, the operator is thinking, *Once I get done pumping out this boat, I am going tie this stinkpot up and offer my resignation.* Even Sid—the great war veteran with his levelheaded and pleasant disposition—must have considered this at one point.

It's a rough job: 40-hour weeks, and you smell like septic the entire time. This alone never bothered me, but in July and August, Montauk gets very hot—humid, too. We had several days over 90 degrees. You can get dehydrated easily, so people always offer you water, which is great.

In those summer months, everyone needs you and calls for your services via VHF radio (take my advice: do not give out your phone number!). One guy approached me at the Harvest Restaurant, where I was dining with my girlfriend. As he approached our table, I thought he was going ask me about my movie on HBO or best-selling book on striped bass, or maybe he'd want an autograph. Instead, he told me his tank was full and asked if I could come by his boat around 3 p.m. the next day and pump him out. The nerve!

*

People whistle at you and scream across the harbor to get your attention. Most people are mature. They're kind and helpful. They understand the value of the service, and they appreciate your efforts. Good people.

It's the young people—18 to 24 years old, I imagine—who can't handle it. I mean, I'm not sure I would have at that age, either. They see you pull up, and when they realize the nature of your visit and that one boat and one man is assigned this single task, they go into shock.

Sure, the kids are nice enough. They often smile and are exceedingly polite: "Thanks for coming. Would you like some water or soda?" But you know behind all this politeness, they're thinking, *Look at this poor schlep. How many horrific life decisions—how many bad career turns did it take for this guy to finally end up in this god forsaken job?*

And the job is not for everyone. People between 20 and 40 probably would be too vain or self-conscious or—what am I trying to say?—well, you're not going to attract too many young ladies operating the pump out boat. Anyway, you have to be a humble and polite, and you have to know your station; gossips and hotheads won't last.

Still, I remain resolved: The job has dignity.

*

As the summer progressed, I somehow did not mind when people would toot their horn in the middle of Main Street and yell, "Hey, it's the Pump Out Guy!" Especially when I had a paycheck in my pocket. And I knew the harbor was that much cleaner because of me—in my mind, anyway. As the sign that Sid used to proudly display on front of the boat, I was "Number 1 in the number 2 business."

And frankly, that was fine with me, It's important to know ones station in life.

About the Author:

Jeff Nichols' first book Trainwreck (Simon & Shuster) , was made into a movie by Lions Gate films renamed American Loser, it was an HBO featured film in 2016. Jeff has written over the years for Penthouse, NY Post, Easthampton Star, Dan's Papers. He now runs the Montauk Marine Septic boat and monitors channel 73.

Jeff Nichols had a lifelong obsession with fishing. While failing at other careers (teaching, standup comedy, photocopy sales), he was determined for some diluted reason, to become a charter boat captain in Montauk NY, a port that once laid claimed to be the sports fishing capital of the world.

Made in the USA
Middletown, DE
12 December 2021

55401700R00115